Grow
Your
Own

Most of these chapters were originally published
in an earlier form in the *San Francisco Express Times*
which has now changed its name to *Good Times*

Illustrations by Jeanie Darlington
Cover by Sandy & Jeanie Darlington
Front cover photo by Robert Altman
Back cover photo by Jon Kinney
Edited by Don Burns
Typeset by Berkeley Publishing Co.
Printed by Edwards Brothers Inc.
First Printing of 4,000 March 1970
Second Printing of 10,000 May 1970
Third Printing of 10,000 October 1970
Fourth Printing of 10,000 March 1971

Published by The Bookworks
2010 Seventh Street
Berkeley, California 94710

This book is dedicated to Sandy for his lovingness,
patience and helpfulness in all ways.

TABLE OF CONTENTS

Introduction   Page 1
Humus   15
Compost   18
Organic Fertilizers   23
Soil pH   28
Soil Preparation   32
What to Plant When and How   34
Mulches   45
Messages from Earth Gods   48
Midsummer and Fall Plantings   52
Keeping an Upper Hand on the Bugs   55
Snails and Slugs   61
Hungry Gardens   64
Transplanting Advice   67
Seedlings   69
Wild Fennel   70
Indoor Goodies   71
Grow Your Own in Five Days   73
Sunflowers   76
Sunflower Puzzle   78
Conclusion   80
Bibliography   81
Useful Addresses   84
Sunflower Puzzle Answers   86

LIST OF ILLUSTRATIONS

1. Lurvie on the Hay Mulch under the   Page 7
   Artichoke Plant
2. Manty   12
3. A Sample Compost Pile   20
4. Swiss Chard   30
5. Two very simple cold frames   37
6. Chicken Wire Support for Tomatoes   39
7. Zuccini Squash   41
8. Hummingbird in the Pineapple Sage   44
9. Bird Feeder out the Kitchen Window   58
10. Nasturtiums and Snails   60
11. Snail and Birdproof Protection for   62
    Young Seedlings
12. Sunflower Puzzle   77

INTRODUCTION

I haven't been a mad gardener all my life. In fact, I really only began in the spring of '68 with a vegetable garden. I had tended a small flower garden behind our flat in London, but this was my first real attempt. And it was the first whole summer Sandy and I had ever been in one place since we'd met 6 years before.

We moved into a cottage in Albany, California, just north of Berkeley, in August the year before. There was a nice size back yard full of dying roses, 3 foot tall grass and 35 year old fruit trees — apple, pear, apricot and plum. The house was all overgrown with vines and looked straight out of Hansel and Gretel so we left it that way. But we did cut the grass, prune the roses, and spray them and the fruit trees with some poison or other. It seemed like the right thing to do. We didn't do much else until the next spring when I decided I might try planting some tomatoes.

I was working at a nursery at the time, so I had plenty of knowledge about all the super fertilizers and magic bug killers. And I was pretty good at selling these to the customers. One spray company even paid the employees dividends each month according to how much of their product we sold. Naturally I pushed it. Fortunately, it was the least toxic spray we carried and was safe (?) to be used on vegetables within one day of harvest. It didn't contain **DDT**. But I wondered, 'If it kills all the bugs it says it does, how come one day will make it safe for me?'

Here's a sample weekly ad from the nursery:

> We've got 'em...we've got the guns to
> murder your weeds, kill them so that
> they will lay off for awhile. Come
> in today and ask for a killer.

And then there were the combination chemical fertilizers, 0-10-10, 10-20-10, the numbers denoting the nitrogen, phosphorus and potash (NPK) content. The box told what the fertilizer was for, and that was that. Easy. But a few customers swore by manure and manure alone. How could this be?

Luckily, I happened to pick up from the floor one day an introductory offer to 10 months of *Organic Gardening and Farming Magazine* at half price. It dawned on me then, that I wanted to learn how to garden with natural fertilizers and without poisons. I could hardly wait to receive my first issue. With the offer, I was sent a handy pamphlet as well, called "Organic Fertilizing — Secret of Garden Experts." From then on, I was on the road to discovering about the mysteries of blood meal, ground rock phosphate, kelp meal and other such exotic sounding things. I had thought Organic Gardening was something weird old spinsters in Marin County did, like saving seed from year to year for the past 35 years and things like that.

At about this time, I quit the nursery. A third of the products I was selling were only making Standard Oil richer and the air and earth more polluted. I felt rather guilty.

In the meantime, I had begun my garden. I chose a small 10' by 10' grassy spot which received full sun all day. I didn't really know where to start, but I thought I should somehow kill the grass. This was before I'd found the magazine offer and I didn't know that I could simply turn the grass under and leave it to decompose. So I applied a lot of sulphate of ammonia, which is a super rich nitrogenous chemical fertilizer to burn off the grass. (Chemical fertilizers used in excess, and without water, will burn.) I later learned that this was a big mistake because the fertilizer killed the earthworms, and because the sulphur residue left by the fertilizer ate away whatever organic matter I added for quite a while. Fortunately the magazine and the fertilizer pamphlet arrived in time to save me from other such disasters.

I now had a 10′ by 10′ plot of hard, clay soil rich in nitrogen. With a lot of hard work, Sandy and I and my visiting sister and brother-in-law managed to turn over the soil. By the time we finished that, the fertilizer pamphlet had arrived. In it I read that I still needed to add some phosphorus (P) and potash (K) and some organic matter. So I dug in a sack of steer manure thinking that would be enough organic matter. And I sprinkled on 5 lbs. of bone meal (P) and a whole lot of ashes (K) from our wood stove.

Then I was ready to plant. I planted a lot of things — both seeds and seedlings. Beginner's luck was with me and most everything began to grow. But the soil was still hard as a rock. Water would turn it to gooey mud, and a few days later it was cracked and rock-hard again. I cultivated it, but that didn't help much.

By then I was beginning to realize the importance of organic matter and proper soil preparation. That 10′ by 10′ plot could have used 10 sacks of manure.

Good soil should contain 50% air and water, 45% inorganic minerals from rock fragments, and 5% organic matter or humus. I seemed to have no air and no humus in my soil, only hard clay and plenty of sulphur residue. In fact, this is the state of many peoples' garden soils. And then they wonder why they don't have green thumbs.

The clay was supporting the plants and they were growing, but I wanted to improve the soil, because I was sure they would grow better. Compost seemed to be the answer. I could make my own humus out of weeds and grass and other things. And I had read that lots of compost would help reduce the toxic effects of a chemically treated soil.

I began my compost pile somewhat sceptically. Would all those weeds and grass clippings and leaves really turn into the beautiful, black crumbly substance they said it would? I added some vegetable peelings and scraps to the pile too, but not very often out of pure laziness. It was easier by far to throw them in the garbage bag below the sink than to walk all the way down the back stairs to the compost pile. It never occured to me then that I could separate the garbage.

I covered the compost pile with black plastic and it never smelled. I kept the pile moist and turned it after a few weeks. After a month, I began to see evidence of a "black crumbly substance" and I was thrilled. This style of gardening really appealed to me. I felt a bit like an alchemist. Later on, when I began to see the effects of this "black gold" on my plants, I really believed in compost!

Meanwhile, my 10' by 10' garden was coming along. Eight tomato plants crammed in amongst broccoli, zuccini, italian cocozelle, bell pepper, eggplant, beets, lettuce, italian flat beans, snow peas, and way too much swiss chard — out of loyalty to an early childhood memory. The taste of swiss chard from the neighborhood victory garden will always remain with me. A delicious earthy taste that I hadn't forgotten, despite the disappearance of swiss chard after the war — on our table anyway.

My parents had always been enthusiastic gardeners. They had a compost pile and they threw around words like humus and manure (titter, giggle).

I used to help my father root pachysandra cuttings in flats of sand, 100 plants per flat, a penny a plant. It was great fun. He used the plant as a ground cover in shady spots and under trees. My parents spent almost every available minute of the weekends in the yard, cutting grass, pruning roses, planting annuals, dividing perenniels, and planting new trees. They claimed it was fun and relaxing. Now I see what they meant.

Working with the earth, smelling it, improving it, watching things grow in it made me feel good. It slowed me down and made life seem OK even if I was depressed or sad.

And so the first summer went by. Some failures, but not many. Mostly great success. Squash to give away, chinese pea pods that melted in our mouths, and the most delicious beans I had ever eaten. There were wonderful sweet tomatoes — all kinds — Beefsteak, Spring Giant, Pearson, Ace, Earliana, Jubilee, red pear, and cherry, all the way up to Thanksgiving. And lots of swiss chard.

There were very few bugs and absolutely no need for poisons. The few bugs I had were controlled by putting ashes on wet leaves (*see page 56*), planting marigolds (*see page 55*), and using a home ground onion-pepper-garlic spray (*see page 40*). The Mexican bean beetle was there, but we still had plenty of beans.

The tomatoes, planted too close together, twined all around each other and broke the stakes supporting them, but we still had plenty of tomatoes. And the hay mulch kept them from rotting.

Mulch, that mysterious word, was largely responsible for the success of the garden. The early summer sun had been baking and cracking the hard soil, and I knew I needed more humus. My compost was on the way, but it would take several months. I did add some more manure and this helped some. Then I discovered mulch. Each month, *Organic Gardening* magazine would arrive with more good ideas to help me. I only wished I could have known it all to begin with.

Mulch is a layer of organic matter laid down on top of the soil around the plants and between the rows. It keeps the soil temperature even, holds moisture in, discourages weeds, prevents a hard top crust on the soil and eventually decays into rich humus.

The nearest available mulch for me was right next door in the vacant lot — dry wild grass 4 and 5 feet tall. I cut a lot of it and put it down 6 inches deep between the rows and up snugly against the plants.

Then I didn't have to cultivate or weed anymore. I found I used a lot less water. The plants seemed to like the even soil temperature. It acted like a thermal blanket, and it looked nice and felt good on my bare feet when I walked around picking things. Our cat, Lurvie, loved to lie on it in the shade of certain plants. She thought I put it down just for her.

A few days after Thanksgiving, I took the turkey bones out to the garden to bury them. The tomato and squash vines were brown and dead from a very light frost. This left just a few swiss chard plants here and there. I buried the vines well in the middle of the compost pile so that the thick stems would decay sufficiently.

The year was almost over and the garden was finished. I didn't think about things I might have planted for winter crops, not knowing then that it was possible. But I wasn't sad. It had been a fine summer. So I sprinkled the ground with bone and blood meal and put on a nice blanket of leaves. The hay mulch had long since decayed away into the soil.

II.

During the fall of that year, Sandy and I noticed how many birds there were in the yard and especially in the entwining rose and pyracantha trees outside our kitchen window. We had been living in our cottage for a year and four months by then, and hadn't used any poison sprays for the past 9 or 10 months. The birds had passed the word around and had

Lurvie on the Hay Mulch
under the Artichoke Plant

already eaten every red pyracantha berry. The berries made them drunk. One tipsy bird flew into the window once, but luckily didn't break the glass.

I made a bird feeder by tacking a 1 inch edge around a 2 by 1 foot board. I tied it up in the rose tree 3 feet outside the kitchen window and we spent many hours watching them. It's a lot better than the Today show at breakfast. Sometimes we layed out a smorgasbord for them of suet, birdseed, oatmeal, raisins and peanut butter. They even developed a snob taste for health food peanut butter, and wouldn't touch that cheap, hydrogenated stuff. The scrub jays were really funny. They came exclusively for sunflower seeds and would squawk and carry on so that they could have the whole feeder to themselves. They would try to fill up their beaks with three or four seeds and then fly away to a rooftop to eat them. Invariably, they would drop all but one seed while they were trying to stuff the fourth one in, but they would keep trying anyway. And there were catbirds, song sparrows, house finches and a cute little thing I called fat fluffy.

By mid-January, I was already planning for next summer. The seed catalogues had begun to arrive, showing all kinds of delicious things I could raise. It was too early to begin planting, but at least I could write an article for the paper Sandy had been writing for during the last year — the San Francisco Express Times. I wanted to help people get started on gardens and not make the mistakes I had. I wrote an article on soil preparation, so that the organic fertilizer applied would be in an available form come March or April. That was the beginning of *Grow Your Own*.

By January 30, I had already made a crude cold frame for starting seedlings and I had cut the grass once. The rains were warm and my fingers were itching.

A few weeks later, I was digging manure and lots of compost into the vegetable garden and flower border gardens. The vegetable patch looked pretty good although it still needed plenty more organic matter. It was a vast improvement over last year's clay patch.

On February 14, I planted some snow pea seeds. The snails ate them all when they were one inch high. The snails were really thick, due to a very wet winter. But I planted some more seeds and devised a cheese-cloth cover. (See text on page 61 and illustration on page 62.) Soon after, my beets, carrots and parsley seeds went in. As the weather warmed up, I started a lot of seeds in peat pots for the cold frame.

Meanwhile I had been thinking about how I could try to restore the ecological balance in the backyard. The birds had come back and were already busy eating lots of insects on the fruit tree branches. One night while out snail hunting, I encountered a lizard. It scared the wits out of me, until I remembered that they ate slugs. And I knew I could order lady bugs and praying mantis egg cases.

In this case, when I speak of "restoring the ecological balance," I mean that I wanted to cut down on the plant eating bugs without resorting to bug sprays. To do that, you invite certain predatory, carnivorous insects into your garden, such as ladybugs and mantids. This is a little hard in a small backyard, because a neighbor's spray program could defeat the effort. But it was worth a try and it only cost me $4.00. The lady bugs and mantids arrived in early April. After eating their fill of aphids, the lady bugs mated, layed eggs and died because it was the end of their life cycle. By the end of May, the baby mantids had hatched and the new ladybugs had come out of their larvae stage.

The lady bugs ate aphids, mealybugs, scale and many other tiny insects. There were plenty of them around. We never did figure out exactly what the mantids ate, but they looked fat and well fed and were very tame. I only saw one or two Mexican bean beetles, and it is said that mantids like them. All I know is that my bean leaves weren't eaten to a lacey remain of veins like they were the year before.

And every once in a while, little pint-sized birds would hop amongst the rose bushes and gobble all the aphids off each new shoot.

The peas grew 6 feet high, despite the fact they were dwarf grey sugar peas (2 and 1/2 feet maximum said the package). We were eating them from the middle of May through the end of June. Beets and carrots soon followed. Then broccoli and chard; italian and Kentucky Wonder beans; white corn, artichokes, zuccini, greyzini, italian cocozelle; oak leaf and ruby lettuce; escarole and endive; shallots, onions and leeks; and finally Spring Giant, Pearson and yellow pear tomatoes. The tomatoes ripened very late, but that was because I had rotated the crop from last year's spot and it wasn't as hot and sunny in the new place. Now I know that rotation isn't really necessary as long as you replenish the organic matter in the soil. The soil bacteria working on the humus will destroy any disease organisms connected with tomatoes if they are there.

I also planted an herb garden containing parsley, tarragon, mint, borage, oregano, sweet marjoram, sage, chevril, silver and lemon thyme, lavender, rosemary, chives, comfrey and catnip. There were flowers here and there alongside the steps in a little triangular plot. Here I had sowed a few packets of seed — Old Fashioned Garden, California Wild Flowers, Morning Glory and Poppies. The result was really a knockout — a mass of every color but mainly pinks and reds and blues and purples. It was like having a full blown real life Matisse right in your own back yard for three solid months. Often Sandy would walk silently around the yard, staring at everything. It was a form of meditation.

We loved watching the lady bugs, who especially liked to live in the upper leaves of the sunflowers. Often they would fly down and land on our shoulders and walk along for a bit and then go back to their roost. A friendly hello. The mantids seemed to like the parsley and dusty miller best for their homes, although one even migrated to the long row of potted plants on our front porch in late August, where he contemplated a tiny piece of chicken we offered him for four hours before deciding not to eat it. We named him Manty and he stayed on the porch until early December, living in a pot of basil. He shed his skin three times and ate baby leafhoppers and a worm Sandy once brought him. On his last skin moult, he acquired a pair of long brown wings, and soon after he wandered away. To mate, then die? The Bay Area's weather is not mild enough for mantids to survive the winter.

I hope this book will help people get started growing their own vegetables and flowers organically. Having a garden is such a wonderful experience.

Some people still wonder why go to all the trouble to do it organically. I think it's much simpler to garden organically, at least on a small backyard scale. People are beginning to be aware of ecology. Organic gardening is something each of us can do to help. I'm quite sure it's cheaper to garden organically than with synthetic chemicals. You don't have to buy five different types of poison sprays and several different fertilizer mixes. Compost can be made for free or for a very little bit of money. For less than $20.00, I bought 100 lbs. each of blood meal (N), phosphate (P), and granite dust (K). That will last me several years.

It's without a doubt more fun to garden organically. It's nice to have living things like Manty and the ladybugs around. They become friends. And it's a good influence on your children. It's a pleasure to dig into rich soil, full of fat, happy earthworms. I love watching the birds splash around in our improvised bird bath and knowing that any bread I toss out to them will be gone in several hours.

Organically grown food really does taste better. Unfortunately I have seen some pretty sad looking organic

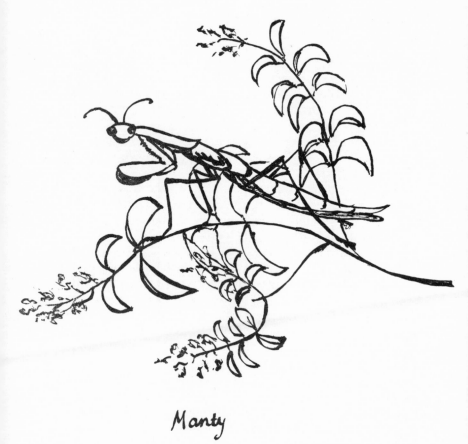

Manty

produce at some health food stores. I don't know if this is due to the problems of large scale farming, or bad shipping and storage methods or what. My vegetables almost always look beautiful enough to be photographed for seed catalogues and I'm no veteran farmer.

Most importantly, it's better for your soul to garden organically. If you use chemical fertilizers, you are disregarding the fact that soil is a living breathing thing. Soil becomes only a medium which supports plants upright. Chemical fertilizers destroy many life forms such as beneficial soil bacteria and earthworms. Poison sprays not only pollute the atmosphere, but also kill many harmless insects and many helpful predators, thus destroying the balance of nature. Gardening organically is working in harmony with nature.

Notes:

1. All of the dates in this book refer to the Bay Area, where the first killing frost comes around November 30 and the last killing frost comes around January 30. But as it still takes another month and a half before most spring planting can begin, the frost date is rather meaningless. In most cases, you can plant tomatoes one week after the last killing frost. Here we wait until April 1st at least. Check with local successful gardeners for the best planting dates in your area.

2. My experience with organic gardening has been with a small backyard garden. This book is meant to tell you the basics of what you need to know to garden organically on a small scale family basis. As the size of your garden increases, certain factors may change. But everything in this book can apply to gardens at least up to 100' by 200'.

I didn't grow my garden to save money on the food bill. That would be pretty hard to do with a 10' by 10' garden. It probably costs about the same or a little bit more than buying vegetables at the supermarket. But I get so much pleasure going out to the garden on a cold December morning to pull some leeks for a nice leek and potato soup, and going out again a few minutes before dinner to get some tender oakleaf and ruby lettuce leaves for a crunchy salad. It isn't the same as supermarket buying.

With a larger garden, you do begin to save money by raising vegetables.

3. Throughout this book you will be reading about N (Nitrogen), P (Phosphorus), and K (Potash). These elements are very important. It would help you to either memorize the symbols or remember to refer back here.

HUMUS — THE SOUL OF THE EARTH

Soil is a living, breathing thing. It is ideally made up of 50% air and water, 45% inorganic minerals from rock fragments, and the rest organic matter, which is called humus.

The virgin soil of this country once contained an average of 4% humus. This figure is now down to about 1.5% or less. The amount of water and air is proportionately down to about 30%, due to the lack of humus. There is no room for water and air in hard, compacted soil. And the inorganic mineral content is up to 68.5%.

Half of this mineral content is due to chemical fertilizer residues that have built up in abnormal and damaging quantities. The continued use of chemical fertilizers and sprays (which leach down into the soil,) is already a serious problem and is getting much worse, as you probably know by now from articles in newspapers and magazines.

Fortunately, it is quite easy to correct poor soil. But it takes time. You see, with chemicals you get "instant" results, and that has a lot of appeal. Organic processes are natural, *and* slower.

To correct poor soil, add lots of humus in the form of compost, animal manure, green manure (plant an area to clover, vetch or a legume, and turn it under), and heavy mulches. And add the right amount of organic minerals, such as rock phosphate and granite dust or greensand.

Soil rich in humus has structural strength. Humus helps

form aggregates of soil particles that cling together and give each other strength to resist crushing, so that there is plenty of air and water space in this friable soil. Humus feeds the micro-organisms, the beneficial soil bacteria and fungii which in turn create a fertile environment for the plants. Earthworms, whose endless tunnelings and castings are so important to soil enrichment, digest humus and aerate the soil. Humus is where the plant nutrients are stored. Humus is the soul of the soil.

Chemical fertilizers put your soil on a speed trip. The normal component balance of the soil is disturbed by the availability of more plant food than can be accepted. For a short time, everything that is living in the soil gets pushed way beyond its normal rhythm of life and of course the humus stores are depleted. A chemically treated soil is almost devoid of soil bacteria and earthworms. The structural strength of the soil is lost, and hardpans form that make it hard for water to penetrate deeply. This causes dust storm and erosion problems.

A forest is an ideal example of good soil structure. The leaves, twigs, and everything else that falls to the ground, act as a mulch and gradually decay, leaving a spongy rich layer of humus just below the surface. It is well balanced in all the nutrients necessary to the soil below and to all the living things in it. All the reserves are there mainly in an insoluble form, and they are gradually released by the action of the weather, the bacteria, the earthworms, and all the other micro-organisms in the soil.

To create your own humus, make a compost pile, as described in the next chapter. Save all your weeds, grass clippings, leaves, and kitchen scraps. Collect some seaweed and get hold of some manure. Layer it well, using some blood meal to help it break down faster. If you have access to stinging nettles, collect them with gloves on and add them every few layers. Their carbonic acid and ammonia will hasten the breakdown process. Keep your compost pile in a sunny spot and keep it moist. Cover it with black plastic and turn it every so often. When it is decomposed, apply it liberally as a mulch or dig it into your garden.

Last fall, I looked at my dried finished tomato vines and felt sad until I remembered that they would go into the compost pile and would carry the soul of last summer's garden over to this summer's garden. The other night we had some fine mussels for dinner. I crushed the shells and added them to the pile. Maybe it seems sentimental, but if this is the way gardening was done up until this chemical 20th century, there must be good reasons. If you take this much care, if you put your affection into the growing of your food, then you yourself become more a part of the living process. So add some soul to your soil and help rebuild the sick soil of this country.

COMPOST

One of the basics in successful organic gardening is compost. You can create your own soil conditioner and fertilizer by simply using all your garden and kitchen wastes and whatever other organic materials you can come by. Compost enriches the soil with humus, and that is the most important factor in a healthy garden. Even if you never plan to have a garden, start a pile anyway and give the stuff away to your friends. Composting your garbage will help the ecology and besides, making compost is fun.

Compost is decayed organic matter. There are many methods for making it. The original Indore Method was developed by Sir Albert Howard, the father of Organic Gardening. He found that decomposition took place quicker if you layered different organic materials.

He first laid down a 5-6 inch layer of green matter, then a two inch layer of manure, and then a layer of rich earth, ground limestone and phosphate rock. He built a series of those layers up to a height of 5 feet, covered the pile with a thin layer of soil, made an indentation in the top to catch rainwater, and left it to decay for 6 months or more. While building the pile, he placed pipes through the pile, and then pulled them out when it was the full height, to provide aeration.

This is an aerobic method. The bacteria rely upon a

supply of oxygen to break down organic matter quickly and thoroughly into rich black humus. The process can be speeded up by turning the pile frequently. There is a 14 day method which involves finely shredding the material with a shredder or rotary mower, and turning and watering the pile on the 4th, 7th, and 10th days. For more information on this, see the reference to the book *Compost in 14 Days* in the bibliography on page 82.

I prefer an anaerobic method. By sealing the heap, that is by covering it with black plastic, there is no smell, no insect problem, a minimum of turning and water, and quick results: 2-3 months for finished compost.

I don't have a shredder, so I don't put twigs and branches in the pile. But if you have a lot of land and a large garden, a shredder would be a big help. Shredders cost less if you have your own power source such as a power lawn mower. Or perhaps you could buy it along with several neighbors and use it jointly.

A 4′ by 8′ area built to a height of 4 feet is a good size for a compost pile. If you have a large garden, make several piles. Choose a fairly sunny location and loosen the soil to expose the bacteria. Start with any weeds, grass clippings, dead plants and leaves. Layer these with liberal sprinklings of manure. Keep the hose handy and wet down each layer.

All your decomposable garbage goes in the pile too — vegetable and fruit scraps, eggshells, coffee grounds and tea leaves, bones, moldy back-of-the-refrigerator gleanings, and the occasional recipe that flops. Most supermarkets will give you boxes of produce that are too old to sell. (Probably a lot of it will be edible, in fact.)

Pine needles and seaweed are good additions to the pile. Lumber yards have plenty of sawdust free for the hauling. The wineries in Napa, especially Charles Krug, give away grape residue free. (They also use it as fertilizer for their

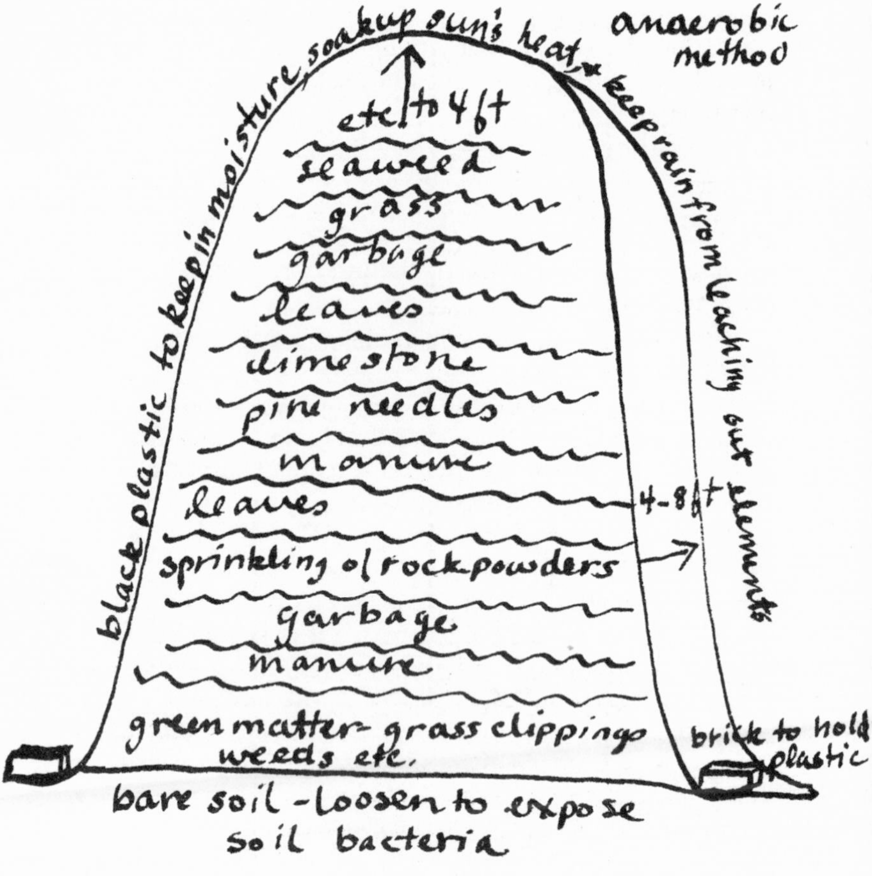
anaerobic method
black plastic to keep in moisture, soak up sun's heat, keep rain from leaching out elements
etc. to 4 ft
seaweed
grass
garbage
leaves
limestone
pine needles
manure
leaves
4-8 ft
sprinkling of rock powders
garbage
manure
green matter - grass clippings weeds etc.
brick to hold plastic
bare soil - loosen to expose soil bacteria

A SAMPLE COMPOST PILE

1. Water each layer — the order of layers is *not* important.
2. Cover with black plastic.
3. Leaves tend to mat unless they are shredded, so don't put them down in thick layers.
4. Add your garbage every few days by digging into the pile, adding the garbage and covering it.
5. Turn the pile after a few weeks.

vines.) You can get a truck load of manure, not well-rotted but perfect for composting, at Grizzly Peak Stables in Tilden Park (Berkeley) for $1.50 a truckload, bring your own truck.

I called the Steam Beer Brewery in San Francisco and they will give you spent hops. Here's how. Take a *plastic* garbage can with a tight fitting lid over to them. They will fill it when they do the next brewing, but you must pick it up promptly. Forget about Hamm's Brewery. They use extract of hops.

You don't need all these ingredients of course, only what's handy for you.

Cover the pile with black plastic. This helps soak up the sun's heat, keeps the rain from leaching out nutrients, and holds the moisture in. After a few days, the pile should heat up to 130-160°, which indicates that bacterial action is happening. If the pile is not heating up, you need to add more nitrogen. If it should smell, add some natural ground limestone.

The speed of the breakdown of compost depends upon the amount of nitrogen available. Nitrogen is necessary as a source of energy for the bacteria and fungi which do the composting work. This is why you add manure. Alternatives to manure are: bloodmeal, bone meal, tankage or sewage sludge. I have stopped recommending cottonseed meal as a nitrogen source because of the widespread use of **DDT** and other pesticides on the cotton crop. If you put sawdust in the pile, be sure to put in extra nitrogen.

Don't bother with commercial "bacterial compost acti-vators." You will have plenty of bacteria naturally in the compost materials. Just be sure to feed them nitrogen.

You may want to turn the pile after 2 or 3 weeks to check on the amount of moisture and degree of decay. Add water if it needs it and add nitrogen in any form if the center of the pile is not finished. Turn it so that the top and side materials become the center.

By now the earthworms will have made their way to your pile. Word travels fast. Or you can buy some red wrigglers to put in the pile. Red worms like partially decayed humus, whereas blue worms like it more completely decayed. The earthworms and soil bacteria release the minerals, making them more readily available to the plants. The more earthworms you have, the faster humus is digested; and the more humus, the more worms.

I seem to have plenty of worms without having to buy any, but you can get them from various places. See page 85 for addresses.

Compost is a wonderful soil conditioner and humus additive. As a fertilizer, its value will depend upon what you put into the pile. Besides adding nitrogen (N), you can add phosphate (P) and potassium (K) in the form of natural mineral rock powders like phosphate rock (P) and colloidal phosphate (P) and green sand (K) and granite dust (K). Sewage sludge and bone meal have both N and P and wood ashes and kelp meal have K.

Rock powders are relatively insoluble unless they are combined with animal manure or compost. The action of the manure acids on the rock powders causes the nutrients in the rock powder to be more assimilable to the plants. Therefore if these natural minerals are added to the compost pile, the phosphorus and potash will be in an immediately available form when the compost is applied to the garden and the finished compost will be a complete high grade fertilizer.

ORGANIC FERTILIZERS

The three main nutrients you want for a productive soil are nitrogen (N), phosphorus (P) and potassium(K). In this chapter, I will explain about some of the organic sources of these nutrients. By fertilizing the soil organically, you are giving the soil natural ingredients rather than synthetic formulas devised by some chemist to simulate the same natural ingredients. And in many cases, you are returning industrial and agricultural waste and by-products to the land, thus helping the ecology by diminishing the ever-increasing garbage problem.

Nitrogen is responsible for the vegatative growth of plants above the ground. With a good supply, plants grow sturdily, mature rapidly, and have good foliage, color, food value and flavor. Phosphorus provides strong roots, healthy growth, fruit development, and resistance to disease. Potassium is essential for the development of strong plants. It helps the plants manufacture carbohydrate. Plants that lack potash do not adapt to heat and cold well, and their process of photosynthesis is slowed down.

Manure is the age old basic fertilizer. Dried composted steer manure is available in every garden store and analyzes about 1-2% N, 1-2% P and 2-3% K. Hot manure, such as horse, hen, sheep, and rabbit manure, is slightly higher in nitrogen. For instance, rabbit manure analyzes 2.4% N, 1.4% P and 0.6% K, and poultry manure analyzes 5% N,

2-3% P and 1-2% K. If hot manures are fresh, they must be composted before applying directly to the plants.

Manure should be stored under cover to prevent leaching of the valuable nutrients. If you mix in some rock phosphate while composting manure, you will reduce the loss of nitrogen. Or if you mix fresh manure into the soil at least 8 weeks before planting time, there will be only a slight loss in plant food. About 100-150 lbs. of fresh manure per 250 sq. ft. is a good amount to start with. Poultry manure should be used more sparingly — about 25-30 lbs. per 250 sq. ft.

Most horse stables will sell you manure very cheaply. They have plenty to get rid of. If it's from the barns it may be mixed with hay or wood chips. That's fine. Find out if they use spray in the barns, however, and use your discretion.

Leaves are a good source of minerals as well as of N, P & K, and they add organic matter. They can be used as a mulch, in compost piles, worked into empty garden beds in the fall, or dug into trenches between rows. When using large amounts of leaves, especially oak, it is wise to add ground limestone to offset their acidity unless the leaves are being used on acid loving plants such as rhododendrens and azaleas.

Green Manure is really a soil conditioner, but it also adds fertility. Soil tilth (looseness) and fertility can be improved by sowing a green manure crop in the fall and turning it under in the spring a good 8 weeks before planting. Barley, buckwheat, rye, oats, pearl millet and comfrey and many legumes are good to use. With legumes, such as clovers, field peas, soybeans, vetches, and alfalfa, it's a good idea to innoculate the seed. Coating the seed with nitrogen fixing bacteria enables the plant to utilize the nitrogen in the air, thus raising the yield and fortifying the soil with added nitrogen.

There is a different strain of bacteria for every type of

legume, so you must specify which type of legume you plan to grow. Legume innoculants are supplied in California by Nelson Laboratory, 1145 W. Fremont Street, Stockton, 95203. Seed catalogues also sell "garden mix" cultures, but these are only useful on pea and bean vegetable seeds. A 30 cent packet will treat 5-10 lbs. of seed.

Grass Clippings are fairly rich in nitrogen and good for working into the soil, as a mulch, or as a compost ingredient.

Wood Ashes contain 1.5% P and 7% K. The potash will leach away, however, if they are allowed to stand in the rain. They can be mixed into the soil or added to the compost pile. They are alkaline.

Sawdust is very low in nitrogen and can cause a deficiency while it decays if it is worked into the soil. But it is fine as a mulch if you sprinkle some nitrogen rich ingredient on the soil before you apply the sawdust. It is thought that sawdust will help neutralize highly alkaline soils. Or you can put the sawdust in the compost pile, if you add plenty of extra nitrogen. The same rules apply to **Wood Chips**, although the bark causes them to have a slightly higher nutrient content. The nurseries sell redwood soil conditioner, but it is chemically enriched with nitrogen.

Hulls and **Shells** of cocoa beans, buckwheat, oats, peanuts and rice are wonderful mulch and compost material. Hulls tend to be richest in K, although Peanut shells analyze 3.6% N, 0.7% P, and 0.45% K. Cocoa bean hulls — 1% N, 1.5% P, and 2.5% K can be bought in nice 75 lb. burlap sacks for $1.00 from the Guittard Chocolate Factory in Burlingame, California.

Activated sewage **Sludge** contains 5% N, 3-6% P and can be bought in 50 lb. bags at just about any nursery under the name Milorganite. It's from Milwaukee's very best sewers and tends to be on the acid side.

And now we come to the slaughterhouse by-products.

Tankage contains 3-10% N and 3-10% P, depending upon whether it is meat or bone tankage. **Bloodmeal** analyzes 15% N, 1.3% P, and 0.7% K. When used as a fertilizer, 5 lbs. per 100 sq. ft. is plenty. In the compost pile, it speeds breakdown, and it is available at most nurseries. **Bonemeal** is too, and it is an excellent source of phosphorus. It contains 1-4% N, 25-30% P. It is more effective on a well aerated soil, so use it with compost at 5 lbs. per 100 sq. ft., or add it to the compost pile to aid breakdown. It helps reduce soil acidity.

If the slaughterhouse by-products don't appeal to you, there are various meals — soybean, linseed, peanut, coconut oil, corn gluten, and cottonseed meal. Cottonseed meal is the only one that most garden shops carry, but remember that until **DDT** is banned, the cotton crop will continue to be sprayed with it. I am told that the seed is well protected inside the hull, so you can make up your mind about this. These meals analyze 4-7% N, 1-3% P, and 1.5% K. They are valuable soil and compost additives and can be used at a rate of 10 lbs. per 100 sq. ft.

When iron ore is smelted to form pig iron, you're left with **Basic Slag**. It is rich in calcium and contains various trace elements such as boron, sodium, molybdenum, copper, zinc, magnesium, manganese, and iron. It is alkaline in action and is best applied in the fall.

Seaweed and **Kelp** are high in potash (5%) and in trace elements. Use it fresh from the sea as a mulch or in the compost pile. Some people wash the salt off and some don't. I wonder if the salty seaweed or kelp wouldn't be a good snail and slug deterrent when used as a mulch. It is also available in a meal form at some health food stores.

Finally, there are the natural mineral rock fertilizers. **Phosphate Rock** (30-50% P) and **Colloidal Phosphate** (18-30% P) contain phosphorus, calcium, iron, sodium, magnesium boron and iodine. **Greensand** (6-7% K) and

-26-

Granite Dust (3-5% K) are excellent sources of potash. Apply the rock powders as a top dressing or mix them into the soil at 10-15 lb. per 100 sq. ft., or add them to the compost pile. The availability of nutrients in rock powders is increased by applying them along with animal or green manure or compost, because the decay of the organic matter helps release the locked up nutrients in the ground rock.

This is by no means the end of the list of organic fertilizers. Depending on where you live, you may find bat guano (1-12% N, 2.5-16% P), dried jelly fish (4.6% N), feathers (15.30% N), red snapper and grouper fish scraps (13% P), NYC garbage rubbish (3.5% N, 1.4% P, and 3% K), hair (12-16% N), hoof and hornmeal (10-15% N), siftings from oyster shell mounds (10.5% P), silkworm cocoons (9.5% N), and wool waste (5-6% N, 2-4% P, 1-3% K). And I could go on.

You will most likely find the following organic type fertilizers in nurseries — bone meal, blood meal, cottonseed meal, hoof and horn meal, dried steer manure, and Milorganite. Beware of commercial compost unless it says organically composted. See the Fertilizer Directory on page 84 for organic fertilizer suppliers.

In the Bay Area, David Pace of the Organic Farm and Garden Center sells the following things, mostly in 100 lb. bags, for reasonable prices: phosphate rock, granite dust, blood meal, cottonseed meal, dolomite, fish meal, hoof and horn meal, kelp meal, limestone and oystershell flour.

SOIL pH

In the old days, farmers tasted their soil to see if it was sweet (alkaline) or sour (acid). I tried it and it tasted like dirt.

Nowadays you can buy soil test kits, or send soil samples to county agents or laboratories, or simply not bother. Generally speaking, if the soil fertility is maintained, and plenty of organic matter is continually incorporated into the soil, the soil pH, that is the acidity-alkalinity balance, will remain almost neutral. And even if the pH is not ideal for the type of plant growing, the plant will still probably grow well.

Even so, I will explain about pH so that it isn't such a mystery. If the pH is out of balance, it will block the release of many plant nutrients. For instance, the nitrogen and phosphorus are insoluble if the soil is too acid. The pH scale runs from 0 (acid) to 14 (alkaline), 7 being neutral. Most things will only grow in a pH between 4-8, and most vegetables, flowers, and fruits do best in an acid to neutral soil, 6.5 to 7.0.

The type of rocks which supply the minerals in your native soil determine the pH. Forest floors tend to be acid because the humus is largely made up of leaf mold, which is acid in nature. Soils along the West Coast where wild rhododendren, azalea, huckleberry and oak thrive are acid. These plants can tolerate a pH of 4.0 to 6.0. Soil is also acidified by the leaching action of rainfall and watering and chemical fertilizers. Alkalinity is confined to the few areas where natural limestone is found, and to the salt marshes and alkali deserts.

What does all this mean? It means that if you seriously suspect that your soil pH is very low (more often the case), have your soil tested or buy a soil test kit and do it yourself. A small roll of soil test tape (somewhat like litmus paper) can be bought for $1.50 from the Perfect Garden Co., 14 East 46th Street, NYC, 10017. It tests the pH from 4 to 9. You press the tape on a bit of moistened soil for a few seconds and then compare the color with the color chart. You can get an approximate idea of your soil pH from that, but you won't know if it's 6.5 or 6.8. Just 6 or 7.

Then there are Sudbury Soil Test Kits ranging from $5.95 to $39.95. Write Sudbury Laboratory, Inc., Sudbury, Mass., 01776. These kits test NPK and pH and give a more accurate pH than the tape. The Berkeley Horticultural Society carries the Sudbury Home Garden Model for $5.95.

Berkeley doesn't seem to have a county agent who tests soil. The Agricultural Extension Service of U.C. in Berkeley sent all its soil specialists to the Davis campus. They've stopped testing soil. I wonder what they do now. And the U.S. Dept. of Agriculture doesn't want your soil either. The only local laboratory that will test soil is Unilab Research, 1220 6th Street, Berkeley, 524-6623. However, they charge a $12.00 fee to test NPK and pH and for an equally outrageous $20.00 they will kindly advise you on types and amounts of chemical fertilizers to correct deficiencies.

If you're sure your soil is sour (acidy), you can add natural ground limestone, dolomite, crushed marble or oystershell flour. These all contain calcium carbonate. Hydrogen in soil makes it acid and the calcium displaces

Swiss Chard

this. The S.F. Organic Farm and Garden Center sells 100 lbs. of limestone or oystershell flour or dolomite (limestone and magnesium) for about $3.00. You will need 5-10 lbs. per 100 sq. ft. and you should start by applying too little, like salt in the soup.

Don't ever use hydrated, burned, or air-slaked lime. These act very quickly and are caustic. They will burn seeds and seedlings and destroy needed soil bacteria. Unfortunately, this is all most nurseries sell.

I prefer not to bother with lime at all. Phosphate rock contains calcium, and I use that. I also use ashes and bone meal, which are both alkaline, and I use plenty of organic matter in the form of compost, manure and mulch. For instance in my 10 x 10 garden, I grow vegetables that like a pH range of 6.0 to 6.5 (beans, peas, tomatoes, parsley, squash, endive, and kale) and some that like a pH from 7.0 to 7.5 (beets, broccoli, cabbage, carrots, leeks, lettuce, onion, and swiss chard). Yet each row isn't tested and limed accordingly and all the vegetables do well.

However, when I plant beets and carrots and onions, I always mix wood ashes into the soil to keep away the root maggot. Ashes are alkaline and probably raise the pH slightly. And the cabbage and chard get periodic wood ash dustings to keep away the cabbage butterflies and worms.

So once again, the importance and usefulness of organic matter is revealed. As a point of interest, it has been found that vegetables grown in soil rich in humus can contain as much as 400% more minerals than the same type of vegetables grown nearby in soil lacking in humus.

SOIL PREPARATION

It feels really good to run your hands through good rich soil, to smell it, and to watch things grow in it. The months of October and November are the best time to start preparing your soil for next year's vegetable garden. This applies both to established garden plots and to new areas. Make sure the plot has all-day sun exposure, because most vegetables really need sun.

California soil has a high clay content and needs a lot of organic matter (leaves, manure, compost) added to it to break it down and lighten it up. This helps in the release of soil nutrients and allows good root growth.

If you're working on an area of hard sun-baked clay, it might be best to wait until the rains have softened it up a bit. But don't ever work with soggy, muddy soil, because if you do, you will end up with big clods of clay that are very hard to break up into small pieces. If the soil crumbles in your hand rather than forming a mud ball, it is in ideal condition to be worked.

A spading fork is a little easier to handle than a spade, because it's lighter and breaks up lumps with less work. But a spade will do. Loosen the soil to a depth of 6 inches by lifting forkfuls of soil, overturning them and letting them shatter into small pieces. If there was a mulch or grass growing on the plot, just turn that under. And if you have some compost, work that in now.

Now sprinkle on a nitrogenous organic fertilizer such as blood meal at 5 lb. per 100 sq. ft. Or get a load of fresh manure from a stable and spread it at a rate of 150 lb. per 250 sq. ft. Too much really can't hurt. Then sprinkle on 5 lbs. of bone meal or 10 lbs. of phosphate rock per 100 sq. ft. to supply phosphorus. And then 10 lbs. of granite dust or greensand per 100 ft., or something else to supply potash. If you have wood ashes, save them for applying next spring.

There's no need to fork these fertilizers down into the soil. The winter rains will do that for you. But be sure to cover the area with a nice thick blanket of leaves or hay. If your garden has winter crops growing, you can do all of this to the spaces between the rows.

To further improve the soil, you may add all your decomposable kitchen waste to the plot, if you don't have a compost pile. Dig a hole, put the garbage in, mix some soil in with it, and cover it with dirt. It won't smell. However, a nurse from Tacoma suggests that covering the area with a board will keep dogs from digging up fresh garbage if this should happen. You could also apply this idea more systematically by using trenches in case you're the type who forgets where you last dug a hole.

By spring your soil will be mellow and workable. Knowing California soil, you'll probably want to add more compost or manure and more blood meal then. But you won't have much else to do except plant.

If you like to work in conjunction with the moon, it is best to turn sod and work soil when the moon is in the barren signs, such as Leo, Virgo, Gemini and Aquarius. For more information on moon planting, see the bibliography, page 85, or check the various almanacs.

WHAT TO PLANT WHEN AND HOW

Hardy Vegetables

By March first you'll be very eager to get busy in the garden. If you didn't prepare your soil in the fall, do it in early February and don't plant till April. But if your garden is ready to go, you can plant some hardy vegetables, such as beets, broccoli, cabbage, carrots, collards, leeks, onions, lettuce, parsnips, peas, radishes, spinach, turnips and assorted greens. The peas and spinach will be finished in June and you will be able to plant the area over to beans and squash.

The exact dates for planting vary from year to year and depend upon the earliness of spring. In the spring of 1969, I planted my hardy vegetables on March 7 and 8. Even though the winter had been very wet, spring came early.

Mark the rows 12 inches apart for most things. Seed packets give distances. Pull back the leaf or hay mulch and dig a lot of compost into each row. If you used rock powders in the fall, you don't need to reapply. You may want to add some blood meal or some other nitrogenous fertilizer. And if you saved your ashes to supply the necessary potash, stir these in now.

If you have a large population of slugs and snails, it would be wise to completely rake off all the mulch and add it to the compost pile. The snails and slugs like it under the cool mulch and they are a real menace to seedlings. I've written more on these creatures in the snail chapter, page 61.

How To Sow Seeds

Cultivate and rake the seed bed till smooth and free of lumps.

Make a slight furrow in the ground with your finger or rake handle.

Sprinkle seed in the furrow. Follow package directions as to distance between seeds.

Cover seeds with fine earth or sand and firm down well.

Sprinkle the area with a light application of fish emulsion diluted in water, or manure tea. Be gentle so as not to dislodge the seeds.

(Aside on manure tea: Soak manure in water, half manure and half water, then dilute this solution to a light amber color. The germination process can be speeded up if you soak your seeds overnight in water or manure tea before planting.)

Cover the row or area with a strip of clear plastic or Saran Wrap. Anchor the plastic with rocks or nails. If the seed bed might be trampled, lay some boards over bricks over the plastic.

The plastic should keep the ground moist, but if it should dry out during germination, water lightly. As soon as you see sprouts, remove the plastic and the boards and water lightly.

The plastic keeps a crust from forming on top of the soil, and it keeps the birds from eating the seed. If the birds try to eat the new sprouts, make a cover with chicken wire.

The chicken wire will be useful later for supporting the pea and tomato vines, see page 39. Rather than planting onion seeds, sow onion sets (they look like tiny dry onions) or seedlings, both available at your nursery. Sow the sets almost touching, one inch deep. Later, thin to three inches apart and use the thinnings as scallions.

Vegetables That Require Hot Weather

By late March or early April, you can begin to think about planting beans, squash, corn, and cucumber seeds and about preparing holes for eggplant, tomato and pepper seedlings. I say seedlings because these three vegetables are slow to mature and do best in the Bay Area if they start off as seedlings. You can grow them yourself from seed in a cold frame or sunny window. See the chapter on seedlings. Or you can buy them from nurseries.

To warm up the ground for the tomato, pepper and eggplant seedlings, dig a hole 15 inches deep and 1 foot wide. Put in a couple of shovelfuls of manure and finished compost if you have it. Plant these three in the hottest part of your garden. It is also good to add some bone meal or phosphate rock to supply the phosphorus these plants need. Then replace the soil until the ground is level. Do this two weeks before you plan to plant these vegetables. They can probably go in somewhere between April 7th and 21st.

The hole will be warmer than the rest of the ground at that level after a few weeks. When you put in your tomatoes, plant them deeper than they were in their peat pot or flat. Roots will form all along the covered stem and they will have a stronger, deeper root system sooner.

Tomatoes seem to produce a much better crop when the vines are supported off the ground. You can tie the vines to stakes, but when the vines are laden with fruit, they are very heavy and tend to break the stakes or come untied. I've had great success with a chicken wire frame 2 feet in diameter and 5 feet tall that encircled the plant and was supported on opposite sides by sturdy stakes. I cut some 4 inch round areas in the frame to stick my hand into for

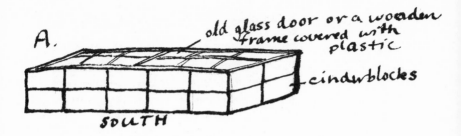

A. old glass door or a wooden frame covered with plastic

cinderblocks

SOUTH

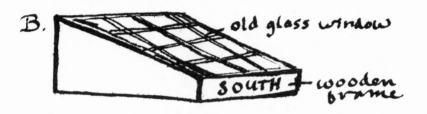

B. old glass window

SOUTH — wooden frame

TWO VERY SIMPLE COLD FRAMES

A.

1. Build up the cinderblocks, 2 blocks high, to the size of the door.
2. Make it draft free and snail proof by filling in the cracks with cement.
3. Cover the ground with gravel for drainage.
4. Lay the window or door over the blocks, making sure it fits on snugly.

B. Build a wooden frame as shown in the diagram. Attach the window with hinges for easier opening.

Note: On warm days, open the door of the frame for ventilation, a little at first and more as the days become warmer. This will help the plants become hardy. You might buy a heating coil (see the seed catalogues) for nighttime, if you live in a cold area.

picking fruit and for weaving the vines through. (*See page 39*).

As the plant grows, the frame turns into a cylindrical mass of green leaves and fruit. The plants take up less room in the garden and the fruit develops and ripens uniformly. You can also use concrete reinforcing wire in the same way, but it is more expensive to buy. Install the frame at the *same* time that you plant your tomatoes.

Put your beans in then if you haven't already done so. Make holes similar to those for your tomatoes, but leave the hole an inch or so lower than the rest of the ground. Strangely enough, this is called a hill and it collects water to water the plants deeply. (This is also the way to plant squash, cucumber, and corn.) Drive a 6 foot stake into the middle of the hill and plant 5 or 6 pole type beans around the pole. Thin later to 3 or 4 healthiest plants.

Or drive three 6 foot stakes teepee style around the edge of the hill, in this case 2 feet in diameter at the base. Tie the stakes together at the top with twine or wire and plant 12-15 beans around the edge of the hill, thinning to 9 or 10 plants later. Do your squash and corn in the next few weeks.

Broccoli, cabbage, cauliflower, and collard seedlings can go in at the same time, if you didn't plant seed. These are available as seedlings at your nursery along with peppers, tomatoes, eggplant and celery.

It's a good idea to protect seedlings against cutworm damage when you set them in. Make a cardboard collar 3 inches high. Hold it together with paper clips or staples. Slip it over the plant and sink 1 inch below the ground. Empty toilet paper rolls or frozen juice cans work well too.

Cutworms go to work the first night you put your seedlings in. They cut the stems off at ground level and wipe out your garden. They are little white caterpillar-looking

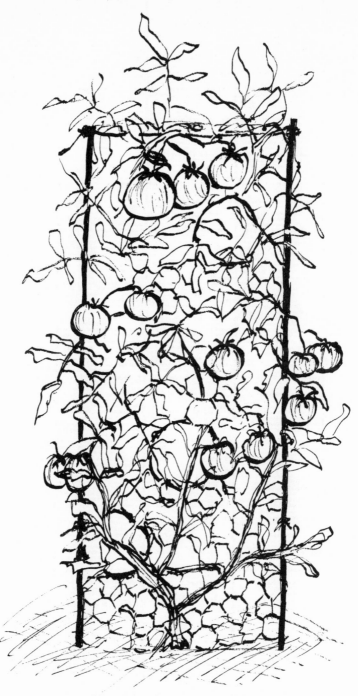

Chicken wire support for
Tomatoes

bugs about 1 inch long when crawling. They lie curled up a few inches under the soil during the day.

Tarpaper circles around the plant also help. Cut into the center and place flush to the stem.

If you're having any other trouble with hungry bugs, try this spray:

1 strong onion, 2 hot peppers, and 2 cloves of garlic.

Grind in a blender or food mill, or chop fine. Add about 1 and 1/2 cups of water and let stand for several hours. Strain and dribble this on the rows of sprouts. Bury the leftover spray mash between rows. This works well for aphids too. More about this in the bug control chapter.

What To Plant In A 10′ By 10′ Garden

This is a rough idea of what will feed two people from June on.

Three tomato plants are quite sufficient for two people. Varieties: Red cherry, Pearson (my favorite), Beefsteak, Red or Yellow pear (small and delicious), and Spring Giant. Or San Francisco Fog, which is a must for foggy areas because it ripens without much sun.

Two peppers: bell and chili. Four to six chard. Two or three broccoli. Three squash: zuccini, Crooked Neck, summer, greyzini, or Italian cocozelle.

Two or three teepees (3 stakes each) of beans. (*See page 38*). 9-10 plants per teepee. Instead of poles, you might plant the beans around a cornstalk or a giant sun flower. Kentucky Wonder and Italian Green (sometimes called Romano) are good types.

One double row of peas. Plant each seed 2 inches apart and the rows 6 inches apart. Stagger the planting time over a few weeks so you'll have a continuous crop. Any common variety will do. For super-deliciousness, try Snow Peas (Chinese Pea Pods). You eat them pod and all.

Zuccini Squash

Five lettuce plants. Plant five more each three or four weeks through the summer. Head lettuce is harder to grow than leafy types. Grand Rapids, Oak Leaf, Ruby, Simpson, Romaine, Bibb, Escarole and Endive are all very good.

This plan leaves room for a row of carrots and beets or leeks and radishes, with a few spots left over. You'll be eating squash, leeks, tomatoes and chard through Thanksgiving. Check your Farmer's or Agricultural Almanac for ideal astrological planting times, if you're into that.

Flowers
Of course you can buy seedlings in the nursery and even the supermarket. That's good for hard-to-grow seeds such as petunias. But seed is cheap and fun. Easy flowers to grow include:

Sunflowers. Harvest the seeds for you and your friends and for the birds.

Sweet Peas. The climbing variety, 5-7 feet, is great for hiding a wall or making a screen. Use trellis netting.

Nasturtiums. Great for hot, dry, poor soil areas. The leaves, which are peppery and high in Vitamin C, taste great in salads or cream cheese sandwiches. The flowers are good to eat too, and the green seed pods can be pickled in vinegar with a touch of mace, allspice, 1 clove and salt. They resemble capers.

Strawflowers are fun and they can be dried.

African daisies, calendula, and California poppies are good for hot sunny places.

Old Fashioned Garden is a wonderful surprise packet.

Herbs
Parsley. Sow early because it takes three weeks to germinate.

-42-

Sweet marjoram. Grows easily and has a mild oregano flavor.

Sweet Basil. Super delicious with tomatoes.

Catnip. Plant an area for your cats away from flowers because cats love to roll in the plants. Physiological tests show that cats high on catnip react much the same as when they're having orgasms.

Sage, thyme, rosemary, chives, borage, tarragon, and dill are other nice herbs to plant. And pineapple sage is a good herb to plant if you like hummingbirds. They are attracted by the red flowers.

All herbs like a good sunny place with loose rich soil, preferably enriched with compost. There is a myth that herbs do better in poor soil, but it's not true.

Hummingbird in the Pineapple sage

MULCHES

If you've been working very hard on your garden, planting, cultivating, weeding, watering, etc., you can relax now because your work is done. If your seedlings are up to at least two inches or so, apply a mulch and then forget about garden work except for picking harvest.

A mulch is a layer of usually but not always organic material laid on top of all the exposed soil in your garden. Hay or straw, grass clippings, leaves or leaf mold; shells and hulls of rice, buckwheat, cottonseed, cocoabeans, oats and peanuts; seaweed or kelp, pine needles, sawdust, newspaper, old carpets and even black plastic. Any of these will do. The purposes of a mulch are to conserve moisture, regulate the soil temperature so it stays cool in summer and warm in winter, discourage weeds, prevent a hard top crust from forming, prevent erosion, and eventually to decay and add a rich layer of humus to your soil.

Since we don't get rain in this part of California between May and October, mulches are a must in my opinion. Last summer, I applied a mulch and then watered my garden deeply once a week. (Frequent and light waterings cause shallow feeder roots and this in turn causes plants to wilt easily if these roots do not receive moisture.) I never cultivated or pulled a single weed. For my mulch, I used hay that I gathered from the vacant lot next door. The hay kept the vegetables from getting muddy when I watered, and it kept things like squash and tomatoes from rotting since they were not touching the wet soil.

This year I tried out cocoa bean hulls which I bought from the Guittard Chocolate Factory for $1.00 per 75 pound sack. Not only did they smell and look beautiful, but when they broke down, they added 1% nitrogen, 1.5% phosphorus and 2.5% potash to the soil.

However, within a month and a half they had already decomposed, so then we laid down a nice, thick six-inch layer of hay from the vacant lot like we did last year. I used the cocoa bean hulls more successfully as a mulch on the flower and herb gardens. There was a smaller area to cover, so I applied them more thickly and therefore they lasted longer.

Ruth Stout, an 84 year old gardener, has been mulching year round with nothing but hay for 25 years. (See page 81 and 82 in the Bibliography.) She never uses any fertilizer except what the rotted hay contributes, doesn't maintain a compost pile, and never tills or cultivates. Her soil has been analyzed several times and has always been found to be very high in every necessary element and of course very rich in humus.

With oak leaves and pine needles, it is perhaps a good idea to lime them a bit in the fall as they tend to acidify the soil. With sawdust, some people like to add a nitrogen fertilizer such as blood meal when applying it, because sawdust robs nitrogen from the soil when it decays. (See chapter on fertilizer, page 25.) Some say this is unnecessary. The other mulch materials I've mentioned should be all right on their own. But don't expect black plastic to decay and add nutrients. Plastic is plastic. Stone mulches are effective, especially around flowers, and as the earthworms rub against them, they slowly add valuable mineral content. (See Bibliography, page 81.) River rocks, smooth round pebbles, or bright red orange bricks from one of San Francisco's freshly demolished buildings are all useful and beautiful too.

The only drawback with mulch is that snails and slugs (*our* most persistant and abundant problem) love to live under it. They come out at night and feast. This isn't too disastrous for a full grown garden, but it is an instant wipe-out to a tender new row of succulent one inch seedlings. (See chapter on snails for ideas about snail control.) However, I feel that the advantages of mulching far outweigh this one disadvantage and I am certainly a confirmed mulcher.

So go out and use what you can find in your area. Mulching may be the biggest discovery of your life.

MESSAGES FROM EARTH GODS

"Who's been eating my garden?"
asked the Mama Bear.

I. April

It's not so easy to figure out sometimes. One afternoon around five, when I was at the library, a bird ate a whole baby lettuce plant that was growing on our front porch. At least I assume it was a bird. Sandy saw a bird come hopping pleasantly along the walk up to our front steps, digging the plants and taking little nibbles like it was a smorgasbord.

What to do about aphids? I tried washing them off the plants with a strong jet of water from the hose. But it didn't help much. In early April, I ordered a half pint of lady bugs from the Bio-Control Co., Rt. 2., Box 2397, Auburn, Calif., 95603, for $2.00 postpaid. They ship the lady bugs the day they receive your order and money, and they arrive within two days in a little box with a screen on one side so they can breathe. That freaked our mail lady when she reached in her mail bag at six a.m. to start sorting her parcels and came up with a whole box of creepy crawleys. They smell beautiful, like messages from earth gods.

We released them that night after sundown according to instructions, sprinkling them around the plants, so they would have a better chance to forget their fright at being handled and could settle down a bit. They don't fly at night. These were old lady bugs as young ones will not be available till after May 15. Nevertheless, they started gobbling aphids and mating first thing next day, so we will soon have some hardy young ones too.

I also ordered four Chinese Praying Mantis egg cases. Their virtue is that they love to eat insects, from flies to aphids to caterpillars. . .but not lady bugs, unless they are starving. They are the only known insect that can turn its head and look over its shoulder. Paranoia? They're supposed to make good pets and can be trained to eat out of your hand. We'll see.

The purpose of all this is to arrive at an ecological balance in your garden, yard, or nature area by introducing more life rather than by killing it with poison. There are now over a billion pounds of **DDT** or its toxic derivitive in our environment. **DDT** doesn't break down, so it's all there in our bodies, and in animals and fish. That thought is disgusting in itself, but when I think of the smell, the delight and the wonder of putting ladybugs and praying mantids into your environment, it's impossible for me to understand why people so often choose such sick solutions to their problems, ones that harm the planet we live on.

II. June

By early June, I was able to see how effective the half pint of ladybugs had been that we released in early April. Most of them died soon after we released them because it was the end of their life cycle. But before they did, they mated and laid lots of eggs. Imagine Volkswagens humping. That's what ladybugs look like when they mate.

The larvae have been growing from microscopic size to a half inch in length and have now hatched. The larva is black with some orange spots and looks like a tiny alligator. When it attains full growth, it goes into a moulting condition, clinging to weeds and grass stems. Then the back splits open and an adult ladybug is born. Its life span is about a year.

Now they're eating like they've got the munchies, grazing up and down the sides of the plants. They seem to like it here. I had heard of people who brought a lot of them down from Tilden Park, only to have them all fly away home the next day. But if they're born in your garden, they're more apt to stay.

The Praying Mantis egg cases hatched at the very end of May. It was far out. Looking like mutants from a former atomic age, they came tumbling out of the little round 1 and 1/2 inch egg cases, about 200 from each, 3/4 of an inch long, and went streaming across the landscape. Invasion from outer space!

The egg cases were hanging from bushes about one foot from the ground. The babies look exactly like the adults except that they're transparent. As soon as they hit the ground, they went hopping and running in all directions and were almost immediately hidden in the foliage. Their legs, thin as silk threads, must be incredibly strong to withstand the falls and leaps.

III. August

By the middle of August we began to see quite a few mantids. They are now 2 and 1/2 inches long and their color ranges from pea-green to brown. They camouflage so well it's hard to find them.

They're a lot of fun to play with. They love to run up our arms and hop about. Every once in a while, they sit back and wave their front feet about in the air like a begging dog. When I put one back where I'd found it, it immediately licked the bottom of its ridgy front and back feet just like our cat would do. I suppose our skin oil made its feet slippery.

The Chinese make pets of them. But how? We tried to feed them. They turned down chicken and cat food and most bugs, but once one took an earthworm.

IV. September

One mantis has made his home in a basil plant on our front porch. He's been there three weeks now and seems quite happy, having shed his skin twice. We say hello as we go by. "Hello Manty, how's it going?" He turns his head and peers up at us with iridescent froggy eyes. His inscrutable look and exotic shape, usually hanging upside down, is like a silent haiku. We hope he sticks around for the winter, although Harry Mantyla from the Bio-Control Co. says they usually die in the winter unless it is very mild.

MIDSUMMER AND FALL PLANTINGS
AND SOME HARVEST ADVICE

Between July 15 and August 15, you can plant seed for later summer crops in any available space you have. Try cabbage, cauliflower, broccoli, winter and summer squash, bush beans, carrots, beets, turnips, etc. Anything that will mature in 60 days or so and doesn't need too much heat. Before planting, remember to enrich the soil with compost and manure and a good sprinkling of blood meal or other nitrogen-rich organic fertilizer.

Here's a way to get a bumper crop off your pole beans. When the leaves begin to fall off and look tired, take off all the leaves and add a lot of compost around the base of the plant after loosening the soil around the thick stalks. Fill a few buckets with manure, add water, stir well and allow this tea to brew a few days. Then pour it around the beans. Allow this to soak in and then give a good deep watering. After a few days, there should be a whole new show of blossoms and soon more beans, giving about a 60% second crop. It's worth a try.

If your onion tops have toppled over, it means the neck is dry and they should be harvested. Pull them out and let them dry a few days in the sun and wind. Then make them into a braid and let them finish curing in a cool place such as a shed or back porch.

Sunflower seeds are ready to harvest when the seeds start to fall out around the outer rim. Cut off the flower head now before the birds get to it. They'll get their share later, but they pass the word around fast. Hang the head up in an airy place to dry. When the seeds are dry, sort them according to size and keep the small ones to feed to the birds in wintertime. Roast the large ones on top of the stove in a small pan for 10-15 minutes. Stir to keep from burning. When they smell like roasted nuts, they're done. Then shell and eat. Save the sunflower stalk for supporting next year's beans, peas, etc.

II.

In the Bay Area, the first killing frost comes around November 30. This means that you can plant fall vegetables between September 1 and October 1. Many good sized seedlings are available at the nurseries: broccoli, cauliflower, collards, red and green cabbage and kale. It is too late to start these from seed. Get them in by September 30. The nursery will also have swiss chard and lettuce seedlings for your convenience, though you can still start these from seeds.

You'll have to sow root crops and greens from seed, but there's still time. Radishes are ready to eat in 21-30 days. Plant beets, carrots, turnips, rutabagas, kohlrabi and peas. For greens, try spinach, mustard, chinese cabbage, endive, escarole, lettuce, parsley, and swiss chard.

You can also plant garlic and shallots now. Separate the bulbs and set each one two inches below the soil surface and three to four inches apart in rows one foot apart. Each bulb will form a cluster by next spring.

You can sow leek and onion seed now too. Or if you wait till October, use onion sets or seedlings. I prefer sets. Plant the sets two inches below the ground level and two inches apart. Or put them one every inch and a half and pull every other one for use as green onions when they are the right size. Chives may be planted now from seed or clumps of bulbs. And if you have large clumps of chives growing, it's time to divide them.

When planting onions and root crops, mix some ashes in the planting row to discourage root maggots. Before planting anything, be sure to renew your soil with plenty of well rotted manure and compost. If it has been a year since you last prepared your soil, it's also wise to replenish the nitrogen with blood meal or hoof and horn meal, the phosphorus with bone meal or phosphate rock, and the potash with wood ashes, granite dust or green sand. Otherwise, be generous with the fish emulsion. And plan to do a good soil renewal program in November or December, such as I described in the soil preparation chapter.

Always apply the phosphate rock, granite dust and green sand along with manure and compost, because organic matter increases their effectiveness. (*See fertilizer chapter.*)

These natural mineral fertilizers should be applied at a rate of 10-15 pounds per 100 sq. ft. There is no need to worry about applying too much as the plants can only use what they need. This application is good for a year or more, depending on how much you grow in how large a space. If you tend toward close planting for maximum production in minimum space, use the larger recommended amount of fertilizer and use plenty of compost all year round.

Plant flowers for winter bouquets. From seed, sow calendula, sweet peas, and alyssum. At the nurseries, buy stock, such as lobelia, pansies and violas, nemesia, petunias, snapdragons and primroses. If you sow seeds for money plant (lunaria) now, you will be able to harvest the pretty, silvery dried seed pods next fall. And strawflowers are best sown now for next summer's flowers.

KEEPING AN UPPER HAND ON THE BUGS

I hope you won't have much trouble with bugs in your garden. But if they come, it's good to know what you can do about them without resorting to chemicals and poison sprays.

The first step in pest control is to have healthy plants growing in fertile soil that is rich in organic matter. Then they are more resistant to virus and to insect invasion. Insects tend to attack the weaker plants which have diseased tissues and an imbalance of nutrients. So if your soil is poor, add compost throughout the summer and be sure to put down a mulch.

Step Two: Restore the balance of nature. The reason there are so many aphids in relation to other bugs, is that **DDT** has wiped out all their predators. So encourage and import predators into your garden. Ladybugs, praying mantids, ichneumon flies, lacewing flies, toads, lizards and birds all like to eat a wide variety of insects. (See page 84.) The summer diet of most birds consists of 2/3 insects, plus salad.

Step Three: Outwit the insects. Here's where your ingenuity comes into action. Companionate planting is the first thing to consider. The idea is that certain smelly flowers and herbs repel insects when planted next to susceptible plants. The flowers: marigold, calendula, nasturtium, geranium and chrysanthemum. The herbs: tansy, wormwood, chives, onions, garlic, sage, savory, coriander and hemp.

Yes that's right: cannabis. Any of the above plants are also useful for concocting sprays such as the onion-garlic-pepper spray I've mentioned before on page 40. Grind the leaves and add water. Strain it and you have a spray to dribble on the plants or to spray through a sprayer.

Although I have a lot of aphids in the yard, there's not one on the chinese pea pod plants which are supposed to be susceptible to aphids, nor in the whole vegetable garden for that matter. The peas are right next to a row of onions and next to that are four marigold plants. I suppose that helps.

More outwitting: Hand pick and remove first generation bugs from your plants. Do this in the early morning when the insects are slow and not very alert. If the pretty white cabbage butterfly has laid her dusty grey eggs on the leaves of any of your cabbage related plants such as broccoli, cauliflower or collards, get to work fast as there are about five generations to a summer. Wipe the eggs off the leaves with a wet Kleenex, wet the leaves, and sprinkle them with ashes. If the worms have hatched and are eating, try sprinkling them with flour to dry them up. When the leaves are covered with a fine dust such as ashes or flour, the worm doesn't like the taste and the butterfly doesn't like to land there. When the cabbages have headed, a good cabbage worm repellant is sour milk. Add a little vinegar or lemon juice to fresh milk. Spoon a bit of this into the center of each cabbage. Lasts about a week. Also, birds and baby birds love cabbage worms, so help is on the way.

The Mexican bean beetle looks like a brownish-yellow ladybug with black spots. It eats the bean leaves till there's nothing left but the veins. Handpick and destroy yellow egg clusters on the underside of leaves. I had these last summer but still ended up with plenty of beans.

You might get leaf miner on your beet and spinach leaves. Pick off bad leaves and make sure there is free circulation of air around the plants. If you have lamb's quarter (a weed) growing in the immediate area, pull it up and cook it for dinner. It's a host to leaf miner and more delicious than spinach.

Curcurbits (melons, squash and cucumbers) have related problems. The cucumber beetle is yellow with three black stripes, and is 1/5 inch long. The squash bug is brownish black, 5/8 inch long, and smells bad. Hand pick, look for eggs, wet the leaves well, and dust with a mixture of ashes and lime. The squash borer gets inside the vine and sometimes kills the plant. As the vine lengthens, root it in several places so that if the center dies, the branches will take over.

If you get a corn borer in the base of the ear, run a wire in the hole to kill it. For corn earworms in the tip of the ear, drop some mineral oil in under the silks.

Flea beetles are little round black beetles that eat pinholes in leaves, especially seedlings. Put out containers of old soot and lime to repel them if you have them.

Hand pick tomato horn worms. They look like dragons. Don't smoke tobacco in the tomato patch and don't handle tomato plants with nicotine fingers. It could spread mosaic (something to do with nicotine).

Centipedes look scarey but it turns out they're on our side. They eat slugs, and other harmful insects, plus a few earthworms, unfortunately. Sow bugs or pill bugs, those little grey things that curl into a ball when you touch them, are a favorite food of toads and lizards. I can't see that they do much harm. I have them mostly in the compost where they are helpful because they live on decaying organic matter.

Ants are beneficial in the compost pile and soil because they help aerate. They do however transport aphids from one plant to another. Bone meal is supposed to be an ant deterrent, and you can pour boiling water down ant hills, but I still haven't found an effective way to control ants where I don't want them.

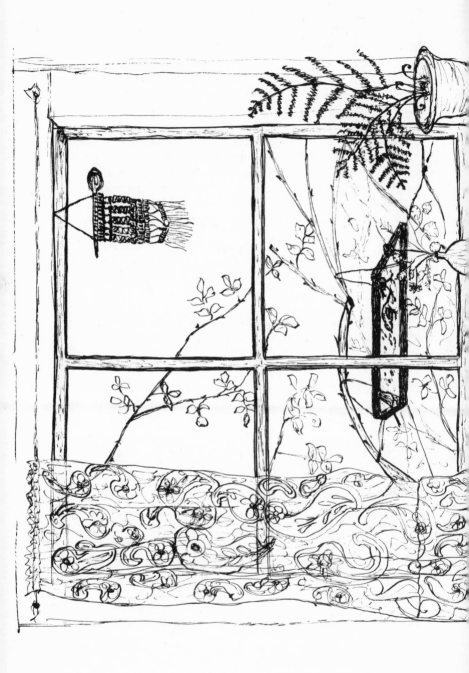

Birds are good friends to the organic gardener. If you feed them seed this winter, they'll stick around and eat their share of bug kingdom baddies next summer. We made a nice bird feeder which hangs 3 feet outside our kitchen window in a big rose tree. We nailed 2 and 1/2 inch edges around a 2 ft. by 1 ft. redwood board. It was all free scrap lumber from a lumber yard. If the feeder should attract cats, you can cat-proof your tree by nailing a long piece of thin sheet metal around the trunk, or by making a wide funnel of metal around the trunk that the cat can't jump over.

Finally, there is a very good organic spray available called Tri-Excel DS. It is made of the ground flowers of chrysanthemum, the ground roots of rotenone, and the ground stems of ryania, three natural insecticides. It can be used as a dust or a spray and costs $1.98 for a one pound can. See page 85 for information on how to find it. It controls a wide variety of pests and is very effective and it is non-toxic to humans.

I hope this list isn't too scarey, but it's better to know what you might be faced with ahead of time. And I hope you have a happy summer of gardening and eating.

Nasturtiums and Snails

SNAILS AND SLUGS

We seem to be waging a never ending battle with snails and slugs. A frenchman originally brought a few to the United States in the 19th century so that he could continue to eat his beloved escargots. *Merci bien pour ca, hein!*

The first step in controlling these little gluttons is to go on snail hunts at night in your garden area, armed with a flashlight and a coffee can. You will be amazed at the amount that live in your yard. The next best time for hunting is early morning. Some people take along a salt shaker. It works, but it's too gross for me.

If you worry about the human population explosion, watch snails for a few weeks. If only they could develop a birth control pill for snails.

In the spring, when you plant your garden, rake off or turn under all the winter mulch if you are plagued by snails and slugs. Clear away all brush and other snail hideaways around the edges of the garden. A ring of ashes or lime around the edges of the garden provides a helpful but not foolproof barrier. Their soft bodies are sensitive to sharp materials like sand, and to dry alkaline substances like ashes, lime and cinders.

The next thing to do is to protect rows of young seedlings with a chicken wire frame covered with cheesecloth or nylon net. (*See page 62.*) Make a frame the length of the row, bending down the edges so that the frame sits about 4 to

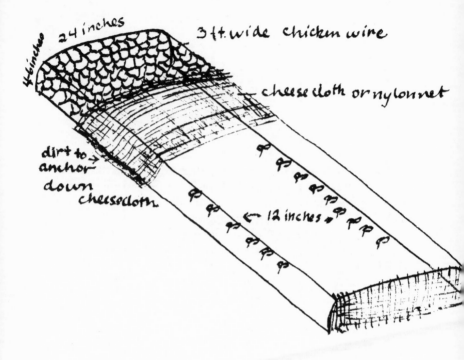

4-6 inches   24 inches   3 ft. wide chicken wire

cheese cloth or nylon net

dirt to anchor down cheesecloth

12 inches

SNAIL AND BIRDPROOF PROTECTION FOR YOUNG SEEDLINGS

1. Cut chicken wire to length of row.
2. Bend sides 4-6 inches in length.
3. Place frame over 2 rows, 1 ft. apart, of seedlings. (Wider chicken wire should be used for rows that are further apart, or the frame can be used for just one row.)
4. Cut the cheese cloth 15 inches *longer* than the length of row and cover the frame with it.
5. Anchor the cheesecloth well on *all* sides with dirt to complete the frame.

6 inches high. Cover it with the cheesecloth and secure it well on all sides. We anchor ours with dirt all around. The sun and rain can come through, but nobody else can, and the seedlings can grow 2 or 3 inches without a care, by which time they are more able to fend for themselves. When you remove the frame, you can still throw a length of cheese-cloth over the row at night if there's still trouble. A frame can also be fashioned from wire coat hangers bent into U-shaped arches.

Slugs love beer. Even the cheapest kind. Put down jar tops full of beer at night and there will be many slugs there in the morning. Snails also congregate under boards and shingles. Check each day.

Buy a pair of geese. Or find a few toads and lizards. They love snails and slugs.

You can also surround individual plants with sand or ashes. I wouldn't use lime in the garden as a device because it would upset the pH balance. Or cover individual seedlings with a tin can at night until they are large enough to have more woody and less tender juicy stems and leaves. This is how I finally got my sunflowers going after the first few were demolished.

If you think that letting snails gorge themselves to the point of indigestion will make them change restaurants, you're wrong. Green Thumb tried it. Snails can travel a mile in 15 days, slugs in 8. Don't underestimate the intelligence of a snail.

HUNGRY GARDENS

During the middle of July, I noticed that one of my squash plants had a nitrogen deficiency — the blossom end of the fruit was pointed. I gave it a good dose of compost, manure, and some blood meal, and I watered it with diluted fish emulsion. Now the fruits are filling out nicely.

Once you learn to recognize the basic signs of malnutrition in plants, it's easy to correct them. Even if you can't diagnose, it's wise to add compost and manure liberally.

Nitrogen deficiency: slender fibrous stems, slow growth, foliage and stems that fade to yellow. In cucumbers and squash, the blossom end is pointed. Corn plants will be yellowish-green instead of deep green. In tomatoes, the tip of the leaves at the top of the plant are lighter green than they should be. The leaves do not get larger and the veins turn purple. The flower buds turn yellow and drop off.

However, if you are using overhead watering, this may be knocking the blossoms off and curling the leaves. (Sun on a wet leaf will cause it to curl and burn.) Always water vegetables at ground level. The blossoms will also drop off if a large part of the root area dries out. Water deeply once a week.

To correct nitrogen deficiency, add manure and compost and some blood meal (15% Nitrogen), or hoof and horn meal (12.5%). As these are slow acting, add a good dose of diluted fish emulsion. That goes to work immediately. Do not use ammonium sulphate.

Phosphorus deficiency: the under side of the leaves take on a reddish purple color, plants are slow to mature and set fruit. In cucumbers and squash, the stem end is narrow and blossom end bulging. In corn, the tip of the corn ear will not be filled out with kernels in each row. In tomatoes, the plants look all purply and are very slow to set fruit.

To correct, add some bone meal, or phosphate rock (not superphosphate or ammonium phosphate!) plus manure and compost.

Potassium deficiency: the leaves turn ashen grey and develop curled brown edges and later a bronze effect. In cucumbers and squash, the leaf margin becomes brown and dies. The blossom end has an enlarged tip. In tomatoes, the young leaves crinkle, the older leaves turn ashen grey-green and then yellow on the edges. Bronze colored spots develop between the longer veins. Fruit ripens unevenly.

To correct, add wood ashes or granite dust and compost and manure. Heavy mulching maintains potassium supply.

Calcium deficiency: The plants are slow to grow and have woody stems. In corn, the tip ends of the leaves are stuck together as if glued. In tomatoes, the upper leaves are light yellow in color. The plants are weak and flabby. The terminal buds die and the nearby stem becomes spotted with dead areas.

To correct, add some natural ground limestone.

Magnesium deficiency: The areas between the leaf veins turn yellow and then brown, while the veins remain green. In corn, the older leaves develop a yellow or white striping effect and in cucumbers the leaves have a yellow and brown mottled effect. In tomatoes, the older leaves develop a yellow color. It is a deeper yellow further from the vein.

To correct, add a quart of sea water to each 100 pounds of compost and apply, or add dolomite limestone.

As for other trace element deficiencies, such as boron, iron, copper, zinc, and manganese, all of these are most easily corrected by adding plenty of manure.

In general, whenever a plant looks unwell, always give it compost and manure first. Then if you can diagnose further, give it whatever else it needs. The best protections against malnutrition in the garden are good soil preparation at the start or end of each growing season, and thick mulching.

TRANSPLANTING ADVICE

Transplanting flower and vegetable seedlings can be a quick way to start a garden. And small trees and shrubs are nice for filling in bare areas, whether you get them from nurseries in cans or from expeditions out into the country.

Try to plant whatever you have as soon as possible after getting it. You don't want the roots to dry out.

1. Dig a large enough hole. In the case of trees and shrubs, the hole should be twice as large and twice as deep as the root area. If you're planting flowers and vegetables, you will have prepared the soil previously as in "Soil Preparation." With trees and shrubs, shovel in some compost or manure and some nitrogen, phosphorus and potassium fertilizer. If the soil is very hard and compacted, it would be sensible to dig an even deeper hole and put in a 2 or 3 inch layer of small rocks or pebbles to allow for good drainage.

2. Try to duplicate the native growing conditions. Put shade loving plants in the shade, etc. Give acid loving plants like ferns and azaleas a nice mulch of leaf mold.

3. Firm the soil well around the roots to eliminate air pockets.

4. Water thoroughly and frequently until the plant is well established.

5. A generous dose of manure tea (*See page 35*) or diluted

fish emulsion will help the plant recover from transplant shock.

6. To prevent small plants from wilting, transplant in the late afternoon and provide some shade from the sun for a few days with a shingle or something. This isn't always necessary if the plant shows no sign of wilting.

7. It helps to sing or whistle when transplanting. Plants have feelings too and they know if you're in a loving enough mood to install them properly in their new home. If you aren't, why should they bother to adjust to their new surroundings and survive for your pleasure?

SEEDLINGS

Some vegetables do better if they are put into the ground as established seedlings. Plan on sowing the seed eight weeks ahead of actual planting time.

You'll need a sunny window, or a porch, or a cold frame for your plants. A cold frame is a homemade greenhouse. You can make one out of cinderblocks, two high, covered by an old glass door or window or a piece of strong clear plastic in a frame. For supplies, visit your local vacant lots and junkyards. (*See page 37.*)

You'll need 2-4 inch plastic or clay pots for the seedlings. Or better still: peat pots. (*See page 85.*) April, when it's time to put your seedlings in your garden, you simply set the whole pot into the earth and it disintegrates into peat moss and becomes part of the soil. Hence, there is no transplant shock. Plants don't like traumatic experiences either.

Seeds to plant for seedlings: tomatoes, eggplant, broccoli, cabbage, cauliflower, peppers. . .any slow maturing plant.

How to plant. Fill pots with potting soil, which you can buy at a nursery, or with peat moss or rich composted soil. Be sure to mark each pot.

Put a couple of seeds in each pot. When they're about two inches high, pull the weaker one out. Follow directions on each seed packet for depth. Pour on some diluted liquid fertilizer. Fish emulsion is fine. Keep plants warm and moist. Be sure to plant more seedlings than you'll need because of loss due to children, dogs, earthquakes and so forth.

WILD FENNEL

Lots and lots of wild fennel grows everywhere in the Bay Area. It's a tall plant — about 6 feet usually — and looks like giant dill. It is dark green in early summer and yellowish green by mid-August. It has ferny feathery leaves, a stalk a half-inch or thicker, and a large upside down umbrella shaped cluster of flowers or seeds at the top. It smells like licorice.

Last year I found that when I put stalks of it under the hay mulch, it discouraged all sorts of bad bugs because of the strong smell. Of course it eventually decayed into humus. And a friend told me that hanging bunches of fennel over her dog's bed kept away all the flies.

If you find fennel with ripe seeds, shake them out before you put them under the mulch to lessen the chance of them sprouting, although the likelihood of that is slim.

And fennel goes well with chicken.

Please pay careful attention! There is a similar looking plant called poison hemlock. It has umbrella-like clusters of white flowers, while fennel has yellow flowers. Hemlock grows six feet tall like fennel, but the stems are covered with purple blotches, while fennel stems are plain green. Fennel smells like licorice and hemlock smells "mousy," whatever that might mean. It is not related to the evergreen hemlock.

Don't chew or eat any part of this hemlock plant because it is poisonous. The root, stem, flowers, leaves, and seeds are all dangerous.

INDOOR GOODIES

What to plant indoors, for frustrated green thumbers with no garden space: herb seeds, cloves of garlic, grapefruit seeds, and any number of things.

You'll need a sunny window. And clay pots and potting soil. You can buy potting soil at Woolworth's and at many super markets as well as at a nursery. You can often buy used clay pots at nurseries for five or ten cents. Wash and scrub them well to get rid of any former disease organisms.

Sweet basil (green) or opal basil (purple) are good herbs to plant. They make pretty ornamental plants and will supply you with delicious basil leaves for pesto (basil, garlic and cheese sauce for pasta). Also oregano, which is nice in a hanging basket. And chives, thyme, sweet marjoram and parsley. Flat Italian parsley tastes much better than curled. For all these herbs, plant about 6 seeds in order to end up with 2-3 plants in an 8 or 9 inch pot.

You might try planting seeds from your spice shelf, such as cumin, coriander, dill, anise, caraway, etc. If they don't germinate, then buy a seed packet.

Garlic. Separate one bulb of garlic into cloves. Plant about 6 of these in an 8 or 10 inch pot, at least one half inch below the surface, roots facing down. They take a while to come up. Each clove will send up green shoots which you can then use as you would green onion tips or chives with a garlic flavor.

Grapefruit seeds produce a nice plant with pretty pink flowers. Dry seeds before planting.

Apartment dwellers can make compost in a large covered coffee can or small garbage can, using vegetable scraps, a bit of good soil, and whatever else you can think of. Read the chapter on compost.

GROW YOUR OWN IN FIVE DAYS:
SPROUTING SEEDS

"Wanted! A vegetable that will grow in any climate, will rival meats in nutritive value, will mature in 3 to 5 days, may be planted any day of the year, will require neither soil nor sunshine, will rival tomatoes in Vitamin C, will be free of waste in preparation, and can be cooked with as little fuel and as quickly as a pork chop."

Dr. Clive M. McCay

The above quote applies to the sprouted soybean. Seeds are amazing little forms of life. Because they have to last through hard winters of freezes and thaws, of rain, wind, and snow, and then must be able to sprout in the spring and provide enough nutrition for that process, the plant tends to put all its energy and nutrients into the production of its seed.

Therefore it is not surprising that seeds are rich in vitamins, minerals, protein, oils and carbohydrates. Incredibly enough, the vitamin content in them is increased about five times when the seed has sprouted. (By the way, by "sprouting," I mean when you take seeds, put them on a damp cloth until they sprout, and then eat them.) The protein can be classed as complete and the starch has turned to sugar, making sprouted seeds a quick energy food.

One pound of seeds produces 6 to 8 pounds of sprouts. Sprouts are delicious raw in salads and sandwiches; or if chopped, added to bread dough, muffins and pancakes; or added just before serving to soups, stews and casseroles; or fried with other vegetables for a few minutes.

Seeds suitable for sprouting include alfalfa, barley, buckwheat, fava, mung, pinto and soybeans, corn, cress, clovers, caraway, celery, dill, flax, garbanzos, kale, lettuce, lentils, millet, parsley, purslane, pumpkin, peanuts, onions, oats, radishes, beets, safflower, sunflower and wheat. It is important that the seed has not been chemically treated previously. Certain seeds are when they're meant for outdoor growing. It should say on the package.

It is very easy to sprout your own seeds. Conditions important to sprouting are: a constant humidity, an even source of water, exclusion of light, and a uniform temperature. I have sprouted seeds successfully by covering the bottom of a glass bowl or dish with cotton balls or several thicknesses of cheese cloth, keeping this moist and sprinkling the seeds on top.

A more permanent sprouter can be made with a large glass baking dish, a rustproof metal rack that will fit inside, and a piece of terry cloth or several thicknesses of cheese cloth slightly larger than the dish. Put some warm water in the dish, but not so much as to submerge the rack. Lay the wet towel on the rack and allow one end to dip into the water below. This keeps the seeds moist, but not immersed in water.

Or use a large clay flower pot saucer and set it in another container of water. The saucer has no drainage hole and is porous, so the seeds will stay moist.

Soak the seeds several hours or overnight. Then sprinkle them onto the wet cloth or into the clay saucer which has been soaked in water. Leave enough space between the seeds for them to grow. Cover tightly with foil to exclude light and cause humidity. After three days, uncover and sprinkle with water. Cover with clear plastic wrap and set in the sun to develop the chlorophyll content. Alfalfa sprouts will be ready in 4-5 days and mung beans (bean-sprouts) in 6-8 days. When they are ready, lift them from the cloth, roots and all.

The same cloth can be reused for sprouting if it is rinsed out well in a mild bleach solution, not detergent. This prevents fungus in the sprouts. Rinse the dish and rack in the bleach solution too. Sprouts will keep in the refrigerator for a week or so in a closed container or baggie without losing their nutritive value.

A pound of alfalfa seed costs less than a dollar at a health food store. A pound of mung beans costs around 50 cents. Cress or pepper grass seed, sold at all greengrocers in England as "mustard and cress," is harder to find and more expensive. But it's very delicious and peppery tasting. It can be ordered from Harry E. Saier, Dimondale, Michigan, 48821. An ounce of upland or wintercress costs 50 cents and an ounce of fine curled cress costs 60 cents. It can also be grown outdoors.

For reference on sprouting:
El Molino Kitchens Cookbook
Natural Foods Cookbook, Beatrice Trum Hunter

SUNFLOWERS

"When Francisco Pisarro in 1532 fought his way into Peru, he found there the giant sunflower, venerated by the Indians of the Inca Empire as the sacred image of their sun-god. Incan priestesses, the Maidens of the Sun, wore on their breasts large sunflower discs made of virgin gold. These discs became the most highly treasured spoils of the Spanish Conquistadores. Sunflower seeds were also sacred food to the Plains Indians of the prairie regions of North America. They placed ceremonial bowls filled with sunflower seeds on the graves of their dead for food to sustain them on their long and dangerous journey to their Happy Hunting Ground."

from *Folklore and Symbolism of Flowers, Plants and Trees*, Ernst and Johanna Lehner

SUNFLOWER PUZZLE

Across

1. They help in pollination.
2. Something that can be used for a mulch which will slowly add mineral content.
5. A way of gardening without chemicals or poisons.
7. Nature's natural mulch.
11. A good crop to plant and turn under for nitrogen and humus enrichment.
12. A type of planting involving herbs and other strong smelling plants to deter bugs.
15. A hot-tasting vegetable useful as an ingredient in a home-made spray for discouraging aphids and other pests.
19. A purple bird that loves to eat mosquitoes and that lives in apartment-type bird houses.
20. A type of seaweed useful for mulch and compost heaps.
21. A major soil nutrient responsible for plant carbo-hydrate manufacture.
25. Feed the _____ seed in winter and they will help you in the summer.
26. An important part of the soil which keeps it friable and acts as a storehouse for plant nutrients.
28. Phosphorus helps provide strong_____ .
29. Well rotted _____ is an organic gardener's best friend.

31. It comes from the sea and is high in trace elements.
32. A small creature that lives in the soil and enriches it by digesting organic matter.
33. Something the organic gardener never needs to use.

Down

1. A trace element.
3. A layer of organic matter on top of the soil.
4. Soil organisms which feed on humus and release nutrients.
6. A crop planted with the sole intention of turning it under to enrich the soil.
8. Vegetables need plenty of _____.
9. Humus is the "_____" of the soil.
10. Ruth Stout's favorite kind of mulch.
13. Corn kernels not filled out to the end of the ear have a _____ deficiency.
14. A sucking insect fond of roses.
16. Home made fertilizer.
17. Ground _____ rock is a good source of phosphorus and trace minerals.
18. A zuccini squash with a pointed blossom end is deficient in _____.
22. A synthetic chlorinated hydrocarbon now found in almost all living organisms and in all places of the earth, thanks to modern technology.
23. A good source of potash.
24. Any insect that eats another insect is a _____.
27. A very beautiful beneficial carnivorous insect.
30. One of the four elements in good soil structure.

CONCLUSION

Life is to live,
Gardens are to grow
Friends are to love,
Food is to eat.
Grow your own,
Share with your friends,
Eat and enjoy.

BIBLIOGRAPHY

Books

Not all of these books endorse a strictly organic approach to gardening. Still, they are helpful in other ways.

Hunter, Beatrice Trum, Houghton Mifflin, *Gardening Without Poisons.* This book is excellent and has extensive lists at the end on where to find just about anything in connection with organic gardening.

Stout, Ruth, *Gardening Without Work*, Adair. All about mulches and a lot of fun to read.

Gillespie, Janet, *Peacock Manure and Marigolds.* The story of a New Englander's switch to organic gardening. Light amusing reading and helpful too.

Matson, Ruth A., *Gardening for Gourmets*, Doubleday. Good advice on how to grow a lot in a small space.

Krutch, Joseph Wood, *The Gardener's World*, G.P. Putnam and Sons. An anthology of stories about gardens from very old books up to the present. Very nice graphics.

Wickenden, Leonard, *Gardening with Nature.*

Cocomoeur, Joseph A., *Farming with Nature.*

Lord, Russell, *The Care of the Earth.*

Rood, Ronald N., *Land Alive.*

Williams, Katherine Barnes, *Herbs—the Spice of a Gardener's Life*, Diversity Books, Kansas City, Mo. A very good book on growing herbs.

Gibbons, Ewell, *Stalking the Wild Asparagus, Stalking the Blue-eyed Scallop, Stalking the Healthful Herbs*, David McKay Co. These books aren't about gardening, but they are good reading about nature's organically grown wild food and how to use it.

Rodale, J.I., *Stone-Mulching*, Rodale Books.

All the above books are at the Berkeley Public Library.

More Books

Edited by Taylor, Norman, *Encyclopedia of Gardening*, Houghton Mifflin Co. A great reference book.

Edited by Rodale, J.I., and staff, *How to Grow Vegetables and Fruits by the Organic Method*, Rodale Books, $10.19 postpaid. An excellent book that covers all aspects of growing vegetables, fruits and herbs organically.

Edited by Rodale, J.I., and staff, *The Encyclopedia of Organic Gardening*, Rodale Books, $10.19 postpaid. This book covers more subjects in less detail than the *How to Grow* book above.

Edited by Rodale, J.I., and staff, *The Organic Way to Plant Protection*, Rodale Books. $4.95.

Lehner, Ernst and Johanna, *Folklore and Symbolism of Flowers, Plants and Trees*. Interesting background book.

Krutch, Joseph Wood, *Herbal*, G.P. Putnam and sons. Beautiful graphics.

Meyer, Joseph E., *The Herbalist*, Sterling Publishing Co. A very complete herbal.

Stout, Ruth, *How to have a Green Thumb Without an Aching Back*, Simon and Schuster, $1.45. More about mulch.

El Molino Kitchen's Cookbook, $1.00

Hunter, Beatrice Trum, *Natural Foods Cookbook*, Pyramid Publication. $0.95.

Magazines, Pamphlets and Catalogues

Organic Gardening and Farming Magazine, $5.85 per year. An excellent monthly magazine packed with useful information and ideas. Write to Emmaus, Pa. 18049. You can get single copies for 60 cents at East of the Sun, 3850 23rd Street, San Francisco, 94114.

Rodale Pamphlets: $1.00 each from Rodale Publications, Emmaus, Pa., 18049: *Organic Fertilizing—Secret of Garden Experts, Control Garden Pests Without Poison Sprays, The Best Gardening Ideas I Know, Country Gardener's Cookbook, Organic Foods Shopping Guide, Compost in 14 Days, All About Mulch.*

Free pamphlets from University of California Agricultural Extension Service. Write Agricultural Publications, University Hall, U.C., Berkeley, 94720:

Home Vegetable Gardening—disregard fertilizer and spray advice. *Growing Tomatoes in your Home Garden. Cherry Tomatoes.*

U.S. Dept. of Agriculture Publications. Write Superintendant of Documents. U.S. Government Printing Office, Washington, D.C. 20402. *Suburban and Farm Vegetable Gardens*, 30 cents. A good publication, but don't follow the chemical fertilizer recommendations.

For list of U.S.D.A. Publications, send 40 cents to USDA, Washington D.C. 02050.

The Green Revolution—monthly newsletter, $3.00 per year.   School of Living Center, Heathcote Road, Freeland, Md. 21053.

Brooklyn Botanic Garden Handbooks, Brooklyn Botanic Gardens, 1000 Washington Avenue, Brooklyn, N.Y., 11225. They sell several of these at Cody's in Berkeley: No. 50, Handbook on Garden Pests, $1.25, No. 20, Handbook on Soil, $1.00, No. 23, Handbook on Mulches, $1.00, No. 25, Handbook on Herbs, $1.00.

Catalogues

Organic Seeds—Vita Green Farms. P.O. Box 878, Vista, Calif., 92083.
Vegetable and Flower Seeds, organic fertilizers and organic insecticides. Natural Development Co., Bainbridge, Pa., 17502.

The following are not organic, but they are reputable seed catalogues, and they're free except for the last one:

W. Atlee Burpee Co., Riverside, Calif. 92502.
Stokes Seeds Inc. Box 15, Ellicott Street Station, Buffalo, N.Y.   14205.
Burgess Seed and Plant Co., Galesburg, Mich.   49053—they have stopped carrying the "hard" persistent pesticides like DDT, Dieldrin and Chlordane.
Stark Bros. Nurseries and Orchards, Louisiana, Mo.   63353—fruit trees by mail.
Farmer Seed and Nursery Co., Faribault, Minn. 55021.
Parks Seed Co., Inc., Greenwood, S.C. 29646.
Harry E. Saier, Dimondale, Mich.   48821, 50 cents. Many unusual hard to find seeds.

Herb Catalogues and Publications

Herb seeds and plants by mail order:
Capriland's Herb Farm, Silver Street, Coventry, Conn., 06238.
Greene Herb Gardens, Greene, R.I., 02826.
Hemlock Hill Herb Farms, Litchfield, Conn., 06759.
Nichols Garden Nursery, 1190 N. Pacific Highway, Albany, Oregon, 93721. Herbs and rare seeds.   Unusual and european vegetable seeds, french and oriental strains of all vegetables, artichoke plants and rhubarb roots, etc.
Mincemoyer's, Rt. 5., Box 379, Jackson, N.J. 08527.
Shallots, Ramsey, N.J., 07446, 50 bulbs for $2.00.
Merry Gardens, 1 Simonton Road, Camden, Maine, 04842, 25 cents.
The Herbalist—Herbalist—Herb Society of America, Horticultural Hall, Boston, Mass.
The Herb Grower Magazine, Falls Village, Conn.

For books on herbs, see the book section of this list.

USEFUL ADDRESSES

Many Organic Fertilizers

David Pace's Organic Farm & Garden Center brand available at the *Ecology Trading Center,* 788 Old County Road, Belmont, California 94002, 592-0305, and at the *Co-op Garden Supply Department,* 1607 Shattuck Avenue, Berkeley, California.

Organic Farm and Garden Center. See page 27. Write David Pace, Box 8082, Emeryville, California 94608.

Zook and Ranck, Inc. R.I. Gap, Pennsylvania 17527.

Kelp

Kel-Min Corp. of America, 301 Admiral Boulevard, Kansas City, Missouri.

Norwegian Kelp Meal, Box 185, Penngrove, California.

Wright Feeds, Paramount, California. Sea-Gro Pacific Kelp.

F. S. Brisbois, Fonda, Iowa 50540, Norwegian Kelp Meal.

Seaweed

Nilson's Poultry Farm, 3217 Fairview Drive, Vista, California.

Sea-Born Corp., 3421 N. Central Avenue, Chicago, Illinois 60634.

Cocoa Bean Hulls

Guittard Chocolate Factory, Guittard Road, Burlingame, California. 75 lbs. for $2.25.

Manure

Grizzly Peak Stables, Tilden Park, Berkeley. $1.50 per truckload, your truck.

Spent Hops

Steam Beer Brewery, 541 Eighth Street, San Francisco, California, 863-1495. See page 21.

Rock Powders

Paul W. Degler, 51 Bethlehem Pike on Route 309, Colmar, Pennsylvania 18915.

Dried Steer Manure, Sand, Leaf Mold

Topsoil King, On Highway 17 at 47th Street, Richmond, California, 525-0741. Buy by the 1½ cu. ft. sack or by the cubic yard.

Ladybugs

Bio-Control Co., Route 2, Box 2397, Auburn, California 95603. ½ pt. for $2.00, 1 pint for $3.00, 1 quart for $4.25 ($5.00 air mail). For air mail, add 25 cents for ½ and 1 pint; advisable outside of California.

L. E. Schnoor, Box 148, Yuba City, California 94991.

Paul Harris, Box 1495, Marysville, California.

Praying Mantis Egg Cases

Bio-Control Co., see above. Available from December to June 1. 4 for $2.00, 10 for $4.00, 50 or more for 30 cents each.

Gothard, Inc., Box 370, Canutillo, Texas 79835.

Trichogramma Wasps

Gothard, Inc., see above.

Lacewing Fly Eggs

California Green Lacewings Inc., 2521 Webb Avenue, Alameda, California. 80 cents a thousand eggs.

Soil Testing

Sudbury Laboratory, Inc., Sudbury, Massachusetts 01776. Their soil test kits cost from $5.95 to $39.95.

Perfect Garden Co., 14 East 46th Street, New York City 10017. Soil test tape $1.50.

Unilab Research, 1220 Sixth Street, Berkeley, 524-6623. $12.00 to test NPK and pH.

Peat Pots

Walter Drake and Sons, 94 Drake Building, Colorado Springs, Colorado 80901. 2½ inch pots, 40 for $1.00, 100 for $1.95; postage extra.

Legume Innoculants: see page 25.

Nelson Laboratories, 1145 W. Fremont Street, Fremont, California 95203. Specify what you are growing.

Farmer Seed and Nursery, Faribault, Minnesota 55021. For peas and beans only. 25 cents to treat 5 lbs. of seed.

Burgess Seed Co., Galesburg, Michigan 49053. For peas, beans and sweet peas only. 30 cents to treat 6 lbs. of seed.

Moon Sign Book

Farmer Seed and Nursery, see above. For planting by the moon. $1.50.

Organic Sprays

Desert Herb Tea Co., 736 Darling Street, Ogden, Utah. Diatomaceous earth.

Peter A. Escher, Threefold Farm, Spring Valley, New York. B-d spray.

Old Herbaceous, Box 2086, Potomac Station, Alexandria, Virginia. Non-toxic spray against greenflies, leafhoppers, slugs, mealybugs and thrips.

Tri-Excel DS Spray, Fred A. Veith, 3505 Mozart Avenue, Cincinnati, Ohio 45211, or from David Pace, *Organic Farm and Garden Center* (see beginning of list for address). Use as a dust or spray to control aphids, leafhoppers, cabbageworms, bean beetles, Japanese beetles, squash bugs and many other pests.

Red Earthworms for compost

Hillaire, Northville, Michigan 48167. 200 for $2.00.

Andrew Peoples, R.D. 1, Lansdale, Pennsylvania 19446. 1000 for $4.00.

Brazos Worm Farms, Route 9, Waco, Texas 76705. 3000 for $5.75.

Bay Area Agricultural Extension Service

Representative for Alameda County, 224 West Winton Avenue, Hayward 94544.

For Marin County: Marin County Civic Center, San Rafael 94903.

Books of Herbs, Rodale Publications, Natural Foods

East of the Sun, 3850 - 23rd Street, San Francisco 94114, 824-2571.

New Age Natural Food Store, Ninth Avenue and Judah, San Francisco, 564-2144.

ANSWERS TO SUNFLOWER PUZZLE

Across
1. Bees
2. Rock
5. Organic
7. Leaves
11. Vetch
12. Companionate
15. Pepper
19. Martin
20. Kelp
21. Potassium
25. Birds
26. Humus
28. Roots
29. Manure
31. Seaweed
32. Worm
33. Poison

Down
1. Boron
3. Mulch
4. Bacteria
6. Cover
8. Sun

9. Soul
10. Hay
13. Phosphorus
14. Aphid
16. Compost
17. Phosphate
18. Nitrogen
22. DDT
23. Ashes
24. Predator
27. Mantis
30. Air

We would like to have your comments on this book. Please address all communications to:

Jeanie Darlington

c/o The Bookworks

2010 Seventh Street, Berkeley, California 94710

NOTES